IT BEGINS WITH YOU

IT BEGINS WITH YOU

THE 9 HARD TRUTHS ABOUT LOVE
THAT WILL CHANGE YOUR LIFE

JILLIAN TURECKI

HarperOne

An Imprint of HarperCollinsPublishers

IT BEGINS WITH YOU. Copyright © 2025 by Jillian Turecki. All rights reserved. Printed in the United States of America. No part of this book may be used or reproduced in any manner whatsoever without written permission except in the case of brief quotations embodied in critical articles and reviews. For information, address HarperCollins Publishers, 195 Broadway, New York, NY 10007.

HarperCollins books may be purchased for educational, business, or sales promotional use. For information, please email the Special Markets Department at SPsales@harpercollins.com.

FIRST EDITION

Designed by Yvonne Chan

Library of Congress Cataloging-in-Publication Data has been applied for.

ISBN 978-0-06-337436-2
ISBN 978-0-06-343478-3 (Intl)

24 25 26 27 28 LBC 5 4 3 2 1

To my mom: Thank you for understanding me.
I love you.

Table of Contents

The Death of a Relationship

On June 2, 2014, my life fell apart. My mother had recently been diagnosed with terminal cancer and given three months to live. And that morning, I suffered my third miscarriage, and my husband left me. He broke up with me over the phone.

First, he texted me. I was outside our building, sitting on a bench with my dog. I already knew something was very wrong. I hadn't heard from him all day, even though that morning I had woken up to what my gynecologist confirmed was a miscarriage. I had an uneasy gut feeling that I was going to be abandoned. When my husband finally texted me at about 5 p.m., all he wrote was, "I'm staying at my parents for a few days."

Panicked, I called him. Thankfully, he picked up. The twenty minutes that followed were some of the worst moments of my life. "We're just on two different paths, Jillian," I remember him saying.

"*What!?* What the fuck are you saying? You're just not going to come home? I'm bleeding uncontrollably because *I am no longer pregnant*, and you're just going to leave?" At this point I was pacing up and down the street and felt—and probably looked—like a complete madwoman.

I knew my ex and I were struggling—really struggling. I'd spent the past two years working my ass off trying to convince him I was lovable. A part of me knew, deep in my bones, that he was capable of leaving me abruptly. And a bigger part of me, deep in my soul, wished for the ordeal of our marriage to be over. Walking away, however, was never an option. I was way too afraid to be without him.

He never came home.

My life had officially fallen apart. June 2 marked not only the end of my life as I knew it but also the beginning of my journey to figure out what the hell it takes to have a healthy and lasting relationship. What I learned surprised me. It has very little to do with luck, the universe, age, or even being a good person. Instead, it has everything to do with the relationship we have with ourselves. I learned that if we want a meaningful relationship filled with connection, security, and intimacy, we have to take responsibility. I learned that a relationship is like a mirror: it will reflect to us the relationship we have with ourselves.

This is not about shame or blaming ourselves. I want you to feel powerful and to know that you hold the key to the change you want to see in your love life. Yes, even if you consider yourself anxiously attached or avoidant or have faced some other problem within yourself. You *can* be in a healthy relationship. You're not broken, or doomed to be alone forever, or forever unhappy in your love life. You don't have to let your attachment style or your past limit you. This is about creating change.

When I met my ex-husband, I thought I was mature and ready for a truly loving and conscious partnership. I had been a yogi for twelve years and had taught yoga for eight. I'd been in several relationships, and the relationship roadkill of my past included an abusive relationship, which I had processed and overcome. I had been in therapy before. I did have a thorn in my side about my father and our relationship (more on that later), but that was a thorn I believed would never go away, so I had adapted to living with it. I had a blueprint of what I believed a relationship should be: find the person who gives you butterflies, make sure they treat you well, and when you get married, you'll have a companion for life.

My marriage lasted two painful years. Turns out that being an intelligent, intuitive, and kind yoga teacher who had been in therapy before was not enough to make a marriage work. I had major blind spots, and despite all my study of the mind-body connection, as well as the *awareness* that I had a history of daddy issues, my love life had become a total mess. That mess is what motivated me to plunge deep into the parts of myself I had never considered before—including my emotions, my beliefs, my fears, and my behavior.

Missing from my relationship blueprint was this reality: the relationship we have with ourselves is the most important relationship we will ever have, and we will have to continuously work on that relationship to break through the barriers that prevent us from true emotional intimacy with another person. The most valuable lesson I learned about relationships from my marriage was that no relationship has a chance if we don't look within and do the necessary self-examination required to make it work. When we improve the relationship we have with ourselves, we improve our relationship with others. This is an absolute truth.

For more than twenty years, I've been helping people heal their relationships with themselves and others. My path to becoming a relationship coach started in perhaps an unexpected place: on the yoga mat. I began my journey as a yoga teacher in New York City, working at one of the most popular studios in the city. I taught group classes there, and I also worked one-on-one with individuals, couples, and families. I helped people heal their pain. For some, it was shoulder pain, while for others it was back pain or pulled hamstring muscles. But for all of them, it was emotional pain, too.

The quality of our lives is largely determined by our daily habits and patterns. We have habits that keep us stable and healthy, such as brushing our teeth, bathing, going to bed and waking up at certain times, drinking water throughout the day, eating well, and going to the gym. We also have relational habits, such as having dinner with our family every week, giving our partner or spouse a good-morning hug and kiss, seeing our friends on certain days of the week, daily texts to loved ones, and giving back to our local community. Our habits are mostly structured to meet our needs for stability, connection, and—for some more than others—fun.

In addition to our daily and weekly routines, we all have physical habits that impact our physiology. Commonly I see people with their shoulders rounded and their heads and necks extending forward and down. This is caused by excessive thinking and worry (which is epidemic in Western culture) and from always being on our phones. It's also a common sign of depression, anxiety, or fatigue. Students of yoga learn that not only is the body a window into our emotional state, but it is also through the body that we can change our emotional state. This means that with specific movement, coupled with breath, we can train our bodies and minds to find more balance, strength, and peace.

As a yoga teacher, I had three gifts: (1) I could identify someone's physical pattern almost immediately; (2) I could find its emotional counterpart (such as stress or worry); and (3) I could teach my students clearly how to break their pattern and replace it with a new one that would bring more ease to their bodies and, therefore, their lives.

Teaching yoga to couples was particularly illuminating. Often, within the first ten minutes of a couple's session, I could see and feel their stress. Their minds would be scattered and unfocused. Sometimes, they would even bicker in front of me. Yet without fail, after the hour was finished, they would lie down beside each other in the final restful yoga pose called Savasana, deeply relaxed and holding hands. Teaching and practicing yoga taught me that when we feel better, our relationships get better, including the one we have with ourselves. Little did I know that teaching people how to ease their pain and feel more at home in their bodies was slowly preparing me for a journey I never, ever thought would be mine to take.

I started relationship coaching inside the same yoga community where I taught. I knew that mastering a new skill takes thousands of hours of practice, and I didn't want to waste a single moment. I wanted to become masterful at this. I wanted to see how I could become an expert as quickly as possible, and I knew that the only way to do so was to work with as many people as I possibly could.

My own experience going to couples therapy with my ex-husband was not helpful, mostly because we were not asked to take accountability for our contribution to the breakdown of our connection. We were not encouraged to share openly and honestly with each other about our deepest fears and needs. Going through this experience made me think there had to be a better way to help people with their love lives.

Because of my deep knowledge as a yoga teacher, I understand the relationship between the mind and the body. I understand that how we feel physically will affect our emotions and how we feel emotionally will affect our bodies. I also know that the breath is a gateway to either calming or uplifting our systems.

I know when someone is holding their breath; I can tell when I'm on the phone with them. I know when someone is clenching their jaw. I know when someone is grinding their teeth. I can read tension. A tense body is a tense mind. A tense mind is a tense body. That tension that we feel in our bodies is a sign of some sort of imbalance, because tension is the body's response to feeling unsafe and out of control.

I'll often tell my clients, "Take a deep breath in; take a long breath out." Sometimes I tell them, "Take a moment and relax right now. Stand up, step outside, get a glass of water." Those small actions change your body; you'll find yourself in a different emotional state. Or I'll lighten up the mood a little bit and make clients laugh, because laughter is such a great release of tension. And then they're able to look at their circumstances differently.

Sometimes I'll talk to my individual clients while we're on a walk together, because taking a walk with someone is a powerful coregulating activity. A lot of people think more clearly when they're moving their body. It's good for blood flow and makes people more alert and relaxed at the same time.

Before I became a relationship coach, I spent almost twenty years studying how the mind and body are one. My ability to prescribe certain movement or breath work—to help clients feel stronger, clearer, and more grounded—makes me unique as a relationship coach.

I believe that the teacher-student relationship is sacred. The iconic film *The Karate Kid* is a beautiful demonstration of the power of mentorship and how important it is to have at least one person in our lives who can teach us how to master a skill. I've been blessed to have incredible mentors, ranging from my yoga teachers to the mentors who helped me transform my life and who continue to guide me toward deeper mastery in my teaching and coaching. I truly believe that when the student is ready, the teacher will appear. If you're reading this book, I'm lucky and honored to be given the opportunity to be your mentor, so I can guide you toward your own mastery and transformation.

I believe everyone should work on themselves at some point in their lives. What is the inner work we must do for an amazing love life? Well, it's not what a lot of people think it is.

Anyone can be in a relationship, but building a great and healthy relationship with someone is another skill that no one teaches us how to master. No one directly teaches us how to pick our partners. No one teaches us how to love when we're scared, overwhelmed, angry, or stressed. Many of us didn't learn how to love ourselves even when someone stopped loving us. And there are many who never learned that a relationship is meant to support their nervous systems, not wreck them. If we want to get better at relationships, we must face our fears and be willing to make mistakes. There's no way around it. That's "the work." To be clear, though, each of us is a work in progress. Our task is not to become invincible. We do not have to become fearless, free of trauma, and happy all the time to have a healthy and fulfilling relationship. And although awareness is key, we can't stop there. We can have all the awareness in the world and be able to perfectly recite our traumas, but if we don't know how to transcend what has been holding us back from having healthy and loving relationships, we'll feel stuck and unhappy.

That is why I decided to write this book. It doesn't matter if you're single, recently heartbroken, or wanting to improve the relationship you're in. It doesn't matter what your relationship history is—or isn't. I'm going to show you why you've been struggling in your love life and what you can do about it. You *can* have a healthy and fulfilling relationship, and I'm going to show you how.

In this book, you will find nine truths about love and relationships that will change your life:

- Truth 1: It begins with you.
- Truth 2: The mind is a battlefield.
- Truth 3: Lust is not the same thing as love.
- Truth 4: You have to love yourself.
- Truth 5: You must speak up and tell the truth.
- Truth 6: You need to be your best self (even after the honeymoon).
- Truth 7: You cannot convince someone to love you.
- Truth 8: No one is coming to save you.
- Truth 9: You must make peace with your parents.

I'll share actual case studies of clients who bravely looked in the mirror and worked hard to implement these truths in their lives. In fact, everything I share and teach in this book is exactly what I've taught to my private clients. Although many of my clients have been women, the lessons are for everyone, regardless of gender or sexual orientation. At the end of each chapter, you'll find both journal prompts to wake up your self-awareness and actionable steps so that you can wire yourself for the change you need to make.

I arrived at these nine truths based on my own transformation and ten years of coaching thousands on their love lives. Some truths may sting a little more than others, but if you open your mind and heart to each one's message, it will illuminate your path toward healthy love and, ultimately, self-love.

It begins with you.

It Begins with You

We cannot heal our love lives without healing the relationship we have with ourselves. Every relationship we have ever had has had one thing in common: *us*. I know this can be a tough pill to swallow, but it is a necessary one. Without understanding this truth, we will continue to feel powerless, frustrated, and victimized in relationships. This isn't about blame or shame. It is about empowerment. It's recognizing that instead of being at the mercy of our childhoods and past relationships, we actually hold the key to the change we wish to see in our relationships. It's realizing that every single heartbreak and disappointment we've ever endured was trying to teach us about our fears, patterns, and beliefs that have been sabotaging our chances of having a fulfilling relationship. Understanding this fundamental truth also means that we have much more influence over a relationship than we think we do: by changing ourselves, we have the power to change our relationships. Taking responsibility for our love lives *is* what heals. It completely rearranges how we see ourselves; we go from feeling helpless and powerless to finally having agency and control. By taking responsibility, we choose ourselves.

Everything changed in my life when I recognized that all my past relationships had me in common.

Your life will change, too, when you realize that your relationship struggles are not because "they" all cheat, but because you keep ignoring red flags and choosing the cheaters. The problem is not that "all the good ones are taken"; it's that you keep choosing the unavailable ones. It's not that they didn't choose you; it's that you haven't chosen yourself. And it's not just that they're avoidant; your anxiety may play a role, too.

Sometimes, relationships don't work out. We all have patterns that don't serve us or our partners. We all have our baggage. Truthfully, we all do the best we can with the level of maturity and experience we have. That's what this book will help you with: it will show you how to grow in ways you never thought possible. The tools you'll learn and the insight you'll gain will teach you how to become a master of your romantic life.

Throughout this entire book, you'll be reminded of this simple yet life-changing truth: It begins with you. If you want a loving, healthy, supportive, and exciting relationship, your task is to keep trying to be the bravest and best version of yourself. You have to be the love you wish to amplify. You have to communicate at a level that exceeds your expectations of yourself. If dating, you have to be completely authentic even when your knees are weak with attraction. The truth is, even if you end up with the partner you've always dreamed of, you're still going to have to face your demons. You're going to have to face yourself, all the time. A mature relationship demands that we step up. It requires all of us to mature past our comfort zones and level up our emotional intelligence. It means that instead of diagnosing the other person, we take a breath, step back a little, and see whether our own role in the dynamic is serving the emotional safety of the relationship. Simply put, if you want to transform your love life, you must look within. It is the only way.

"Everyone Cheats"

When Jennifer came to me, she was a successful thirty-seven-year-old with a career in politics and two young sons. Jennifer is extremely intelligent, attractive, and highly self-sufficient. Her struggle was that every man she had been with had cheated on her.

Jennifer was committed to two beliefs: (1) men cheat and therefore cannot be trusted, and (2) she wasn't capable of being in a healthy relationship. She faced a hefty internal conflict: on the one hand, she had convinced herself that she was better off alone, and yet on the other hand, she desperately wanted to be in a lasting, healthy partnership. This was an inner battle Jennifer had been fighting for many years.

Jennifer's desire to be in a relationship often overpowered her fear of being in a relationship, and she started seeing Tony, a kind, supportive, honest, and responsible man—and a father, too. I paid very close attention to his behavior to see whether it exhibited any signs of dysfunction, but based on Jennifer's detailed reports to me about their courtship, I could not find any.

When they started to spend more time together and officially became a couple, that's when Jennifer, not Tony, started to unravel. Jennifer was a walking trigger ready to implode. She was obsessive and jealous, despite Tony's transparency, and would go into a spiral every time Tony would even speak to a woman. In these states, her mind would distort reality, and she would convince herself that she was justified in telling Tony how to conduct some of his friendships. She would then create an entire script of what she would say to him so that "he could understand" why she wasn't comfortable with him talking to other women.

During a Zoom session, I could see that her nervous system was very dysregulated. Her shoulders were up by her ears, her jaw was clenched, and she was speaking very fast and loudly about how Tony hadn't texted her back yet about plans for that weekend. (It was only Thursday, and he always texted her back.)

As I listened to her, I felt my own body become tense and flooded with anxiety. I had to act fast to regain control of our session. "Okay, hold up, Jennifer," I said. "This has nothing to do with Tony and everything to do with you."

"But—" she replied. Her body became even more rigid and tense.

"No," I interrupted. "You're about to gravely sabotage this, and I know you don't want to. So please take a deep breath," I said, taking a deep breath myself.

I watched as she sucked a big inhalation through her nose. "That's right, now slowly exhale through your mouth," I gently encouraged her.

I watched Jennifer as her body softened, and I felt my own nervous system relax, too.

"Okay, please take out a piece of paper and a pen."

In the hour that followed, I had Jennifer write down in detail every warning sign she ignored in her past relationships with men who betrayed her. Suffice it to say, the list was very long. The red flags on her list included "alcoholic," "cheated on their exes," "didn't talk to their children," "anger management issues," "couldn't keep a job." These were all red flags that she discovered within the first couple months of dating these men.

"The problem is not that all men cheat, Jennifer. You've just been choosing the cheaters. You've been attracted to men who've had a lot of substantial, unaddressed problems, and that is why you have a turbulent relationship past. Now, please write down how *you* contributed to the dysfunction of these relationships."

By the end of our session, Jennifer had written down an entire page filled with examples of how she contributed to the problems of her past relationships: from drinking too much and picking fights, to being manipulative, to needing excessive reassurance, to being a doormat, to not communicating any of her needs.

I knew of course that she and I would have to explore why she repeatedly engaged in these unhealthy behaviors, but first I had to wake her up from her self-sabotaging thought process. Without first taking responsibility, Jennifer would never be in the relationship she deserved to be in. Without accountability, nothing would change.

"Wow," Jennifer said after thoroughly reviewing her notes from our session. "I just realized something. I guess I've always been so afraid that I'm not enough—that I would never be enough for a man to stay. That somehow I didn't deserve a healthy relationship."

This was the breakthrough that would transform Jennifer's love life.

Everyone Is Afraid They're Not Good Enough

When I was eleven years old, my father, a psychiatrist, published a book called *The Difficult Child*. It was quickly touted as one of the more influential books on child psychology of its time and was placed in bookstores next to books by child psychology legends like Dr. Spock. My father was a guest on *The Oprah Winfrey Show* twice: once to promote and discuss his book, and the second time because he had become Oprah's go-to expert on various issues regarding children.

What was the book about? Me.

As a baby, I cried all the time and wouldn't adhere to a steady circadian rhythm. As a toddler, I needed a ton of structure, hated the way certain fabrics felt on my skin, and would eat only bologna sandwiches for lunch and spaghetti with meat sauce for dinner for months on end. I also had tantrums all the time. My sisters, in contrast, were more "normal"; one was much older, and the other sister, also older than me, had a much quieter nature. My father, being a child psychiatrist, wanted to understand *why* I behaved this way—why I was the child at the park who with "no apparent trigger" would go ballistic, screaming, crying, and sending my mom into a panic as she tried to console me. (She was always successful, eventually.) So, he put me under a microscope, studied me, and diagnosed me as a "difficult child."

My father wrote that "difficult children" are born that way, thereby reassuring parents that they are not failures. He gave parents tools on how to deal with "difficult children," which included structure, specific communication, and more. And finally, he wrote that I had other qualities: I was funny, imaginative, and smart, and socialized well with other children (so not all was lost!). He then added that by the time I was eleven, I actually got over being "difficult" and was a well-adjusted "normal" kid, which gave the readers something to look forward to with their own difficult children.

But even though I outgrew being "difficult," the identity was a tough one to shake. I was referred to that way for my whole childhood, and even into my young adulthood, I would meet parents who, after learning my name, would flip out with a gleeful "OMG, I read your dad's book!"

I wasn't Jillian. I was *difficult*.

This is how I came to feel I was not enough.

In order to heal our love lives and learn how to cocreate a healthy relationship with someone, we must first understand that *everyone* is afraid that they are not good enough in some way: not pretty enough, not smart enough, not skinny enough, not cool enough, not rich enough, not sexy enough, not successful enough, not easy enough, not funny enough. And we're especially afraid of not being enough for the person we're in a relationship with or even simply dating. It doesn't matter what your attachment style is—*no one* wants to be rejected or abandoned, and we will do almost anything to prevent it from happening to us. We'll cling, lie, please, avoid, yell, cry, shut down, pretend to be someone we're not, strategize, manipulate, isolate, or end things first just so we don't have to feel the immense pain of someone losing interest in us or falling out of love with us.

As we continued to work together, my client Jennifer did decide to end her relationship with Tony because, as much as she cared about him—and in spite of the fact that he didn't cheat or exhibit the toxic behaviors of Jennifer's previous partners—the two weren't aligned on some key goals. He wanted more children; she did not. He wanted to move to another town; she did not. But unlike with her toxic past relationships, she exited this one clear-minded and grounded. Instead of clinging to a relationship that wasn't right for her because she was too afraid to be alone, she decided that being alone was far better and healthier than remaining in a relationship that wasn't the right fit.

It's true that Tony represented a better partner than her previous few, since he wasn't deeply dysfunctional, but he still wasn't right for her. The important thing was that Jennifer now understood she deserved a healthy relationship with the right partner. This was huge growth for Jennifer. For the first time, she ended a relationship and embraced being alone until it was time to get back out there again and meet the right person—for her. For the first time in her love life, she was choosing herself.

I helped Jennifer to find meaningful ways to meet her needs and nurture her relationship with herself instead of obsessing about finding a man (I'll give you much more detail in Truth 4). She started new projects, worked on her garden, and spent more quality time with her children. Historically quite reactive, Jennifer practiced mindfulness by taking deep breaths before she reacted to triggers. She learned that peace, communication, and honesty were now her most important values, and she committed herself to remaining single until she met someone who shared those values. Jennifer's greatest strength was her personal responsibility. She was always willing to look in the mirror, self-reflect, and be impressively honest with me and, most important, with herself. This strength led her to change the way she chose men and transform how she showed up in her relationships. In the past, she would easily commit to the first guy she had some connection with. When she started dating again during our work together, she made a promise to herself to get involved with someone only if he shared her values of peace, open communication, and honesty. I'll never forget when she said to me, "Jillian, I'll wait for however many weeks, months, or years it takes to meet a good man who shares my values. In the meantime, I'll focus on my kids, work, and my amazing girlfriends." My eyes welled up with tears. This was a huge victory for a woman who once believed all men cheated and who also feared being single. By taking ownership of her choices and her behavior, Jennifer learned how to choose herself. Turns out it took only a few months for her to meet the man she continues to build a healthy, secure relationship with today.

A huge part of the healing process is learning how to accept ourselves in spite of our shortcomings. Healing ourselves relationally means that, even though we are guaranteed to have moments when we feel insecure and not enough, we learn how to respond to our fears differently, so that they no longer overpower and define our relationships. The first step, then, is to understand *how* our personal struggles manifest into patterns that negatively impact our love lives. We have to understand the ways in which we struggle to feel we are enough and how our fear impacts our relationships. If you want to understand your patterns, you need to know what you habitually do and the choices you make when you feel insecure and afraid that love might be withheld from you or that you might not be chosen by someone you want.

When we're committed to being in a healthy relationship, we don't play games. It's really that simple.

Turn Your Relationship Around

"He wants to separate for a few months to see if being apart is what's best," she said, sobbing, within the first ten minutes of our Zoom session.

"Why does he want to separate?" I asked.

"Because he said we've been trying for over a year to work on our relationship, but he thinks it's not working. I keep telling him it's because he's not trying."

Christina is a pretty thirty-four-year-old massage therapist who lives in Brooklyn. She's stylish, smart, witty, and cool. She loves yoga, art, travel, and long dinners with friends where they talk about love and the meaning of life. I could've seen myself being friends with her in the real world—especially when I was a yoga teacher living in Brooklyn. She felt like my kind of people. She came to me anxious and devastated that her husband of four years, Brad, had requested a trial separation. Our first session was her basically venting and me lending a sympathetic ear.

"Jillian," she said sharply in between tears. "He's totally avoidant. He won't communicate. Every time I want to talk about a problem, he just makes some excuse about why he's too busy to talk about it. I want to fix our marriage. I want to fight for our relationship, but I can't do it alone."

I believed what Christina was telling me, and I wanted to say, "Damn straight you can't do it alone! And fuck him! He's gotta get over that avoidant bullshit and step up."

Thankfully, I didn't say that. Truth is, it's easy to believe a client's story, and I'm the kind of coach who will always have her client's back. But having their back isn't about agreeing with them, it's about helping them. And in that moment I had to remember my wise mentor's teachings: don't project your personal experience onto your client, always question the story they tell themselves, and remember that there's always another side to the story (except in cases of violence and abuse). I understood Christina and got her frustration, but the wise teacher in me knew there must be more to this story. I didn't doubt her husband's issues, but as I dug a little deeper with Christina, I wondered to myself, *Could she be contributing to what's not working here?*

"Tell me about what hasn't been working," I said calmly.

"We first met years ago through friends, but nothing ever happened. Then like five years later, we ran into each other at a dinner with mutual friends. We instantly connected and started dating immediately after that night. We fell in love quickly. I just felt so comfortable around him—so wanted by him. I felt chosen in a way I have never felt chosen before. After a year and a half, we got married, and everything was great for the first two years. We were happy! But then he started to pull away . . ."

"What was happening when he started to pull away?" I interrupted.

"I don't know. I guess this is when we started to fight a lot. He was getting really busy at work—he had started his own business and has an incredible work ethic. I always loved supporting his dreams, but I also started to feel less important as he got busier and had less time for us. I like my work, too, but I prefer more balance in my life."

"I understand how that shift from getting so much attention from him to not as much would make you feel anxious," I reassured her.

"Yeah, I guess I did get anxious about it, but also really angry."

"How so?" I asked.

"I would get annoyed," she quickly replied.

"And then what?" I asked, practically sitting on the edge of my seat. As soon as Christina admitted to her anger and annoyance, I just *knew* I was about to uncover some of her dysfunctional relationship behavior. Being a coach is like being a detective who's trying to crack a big case. Anyone who wants to truly help someone save their relationship has to keep asking questions and digging through their client's emotional states, stories, and biases to get to the truth. Human beings are complicated creatures, which makes every case hard to solve. I had to listen intently to every detail Christina shared.

"Well, when he would call me from work, I wouldn't answer. Not because I was busy, but to . . . I guess, give him a taste of his own medicine?" She gave me a look as though she were a kid who had just been caught with her hand in the cookie jar. "I know that sounds bad, but I was so hurt. He's not a good communicator—he likes things to be easy, and whenever I bring up my grievances, he just ends up pulling away. Which then makes me even more upset. Until eventually, I would explode with frustration every time I would feel him getting distant."

Although I was both grateful for and impressed with Christina's insight and radical honesty with me, I knew that I was getting only her side of the story. Typically, when I work with someone who needs help with their relationship, I'll request to meet with their partner at least one time. Unfortunately, her husband, Brad, wasn't willing to do a session with me or even with the three of us. He felt he had been to enough therapists and counselors and was done. I couldn't blame him. If nothing was working, I would be done, too.

Seeing the two of them together would have been ideal for my work with Christina. But I only had her. My job was to help Christina change *her* pattern and hope that, as she practiced being the change she wished to see in her marriage, her marriage would eventually improve.

I was super up-front with her.

"There is no doubt in my mind that Brad hasn't been the best communicator with you and that you're hurt, Christina. But I only have you, so if you want to try to change your relationship for the better, you have to change some of your behavior. It begins with you. No matter how afraid, insecure, or frustrated we may feel, when we're committed to being in a healthy relationship, we don't play games, and we communicate. It's not always easy, but it's really that simple."

She paused, listening.

Christina's struggle with Brad was not an uncommon one. When we're in a relationship, we want to feel like our partner's number one. We want our relationship with them to be their priority. As soon as something else becomes a bigger focal point than the relationship—which was the case with Brad and his growing business—we won't feel as significant to our partner as we once did. And that's when we start to panic. Our survival instincts kick in, and consequently, many of us will start to play manipulative games in a desperate effort to regain the control we feel we've lost in the relationship. Most of us, if we're honest with ourselves, would admit that at some point in a relationship, we've withheld affection and our love in an attempt to get more of our partner's attention. This was Christina's strategy. She thought, *Maybe if I pretend I don't give a shit and play hard to get by deliberately ignoring his calls, he'll come running back to me.* The truth is, if she wanted more of his attention, she needed a different strategy.

"Christina," I said directly. "You're terrified that your husband, the man you sleep next to every night, the man you've bared your soul to and have committed your life to, isn't in love with you anymore. You've been afraid of this for more than a year. I *know* this fear. I've been you. I also know that when we're afraid, we act out. He is no angel—trust me, I know. But you've played a role in this, too, and you're never going to get him to come closer to you by punishing him with unanswered calls or fighting with him. I want you to feel heard, Christina. But I also want you to hear *him*."

She started to cry. "But how do I even do that?"

"Do you still love him?" I asked.

"Yes," she said between tears. "He's a very special person. A good man."

I was touched by her vulnerability.

"Then I'm going to teach you," I replied.

In the weeks that followed, I coached Christina extensively on how to show up differently in her relationship. When Christina first came to me, she believed that all of her marital problems were caused by Brad being too busy and pulling away whenever things got hard. In her eyes, he was the saboteur of their relationship. But in the sessions that followed, Christina's role in their disconnection became clearer.

Brad would often try to connect with her, only to be rejected. She would scroll social media when he would try to tell her a story about what happened at work. He would call her multiple times a day while on a business trip only to be met with her coldness or a complaint that he wasn't calling her enough. When I pointed these things out to Christina, I was prepared for her defensiveness but was relieved when I didn't get it. Christina was willing to see things differently. She was willing to see that she and her partner were part of a dynamic, and in their case, there wasn't a victim or a villain—just two people who didn't know how to stay connected through challenges.

So I taught Christina how to build a bridge back to her husband.

Christina came to me because she was desperately trying to prevent her spouse from leaving her. The narrative she had was that her husband had been abandoning her and their relationship and that he and his lack of communication were the root of their problems. Deep down, she felt unlovable, insecure, and confused about why his feelings for her had changed. She felt unchosen. As a result, she would lash out with coldness and complaints and refuse to honestly communicate with him.

She became obsessed with her needs and didn't think about his.

I gave her a thirty-day challenge to meet Brad's core needs for love, security, and fun. This meant she had to love him the way she did in the first two years of their relationship and make him feel wanted, chosen, and appreciated the way she used to. Of course, I didn't want Christina to abandon her needs in the process, so we checked in multiple times a week to evaluate whether her treating Brad differently would cause him to feel seen and be inspired to change, too. If it didn't, I knew I would have to help Christina move on.

Thankfully, I never had to do that. As I hoped, Brad stopped talking about separation, and nineteen days into the thirty-day challenge, he agreed to see me for a few couples sessions. With my help, they started to communicate more honestly with each other about their pain, resentment, and fears. He started planning date nights and reassuring Christina more when she felt disconnected because he would have to work all weekend. By the end of the thirty days, he and Christina were planning weekend getaways.

This was a happy ending, but it was nothing like the movies. There were a lot of tears, a lot of uncomfortable feelings, and a lot of fear. But Christina knew that she had a choice: continue to blame Brad, or take her power back and become the change she wished to see in her marriage. If it didn't work, at least she could look in the mirror and know she had stepped up. And that is a much better story than a story of abandonment.

Identifying Patterns

On Instagram, someone once asked me, "How do I stop being a therapist to all my partners?"

I responded, "When you realize that you don't have to heal, fix, or rescue someone in order to feel significant and worthy, you will start choosing partners who do not need to be saved."

We all have patterns that do not serve our romantic lives, and we're all working on something. For some of us, such as the person who messaged me on Instagram, our fear of not being enough will motivate us to figure out a way to be *needed* in our relationships. So instead of looking for a partner, we search for a project—someone we can fix, so we can be the hero and they can be dependent on us and never leave us. I'm here to remind you that no matter how complex your particular pattern feels, you don't need to be perfect, and you don't have to heal every childhood trauma in order to be enough, happy, and fulfilled in a relationship. You need to be aware, and you need to be willing to do things differently. If we want to grow and heal, we don't get a pass on looking at ourselves in the mirror. Regardless of our past life experiences or the length of our relationship—whether it's been two weeks or twenty years—we all have to work hard not to behave like children when we're triggered. Everyone has to work hard to heal parts of their pasts, and we all have to work hard to be accountable when we want to blame. Being in a relationship means we have to open up, speak up, and break patterns, because even with the right person, we'll have to face ourselves. And yes, some of us have more work to do than others, but don't let that discourage you. I've said it before and I will say it again: No one teaches us how to love when we're scared, overwhelmed, angry, or stressed. No one teaches us how to pick our partners; no one teaches us that our childhood conditioning shows up in our adult relationships. No one teaches us what it means to be a good partner—or how to give our hearts to good people and protect them from not-so-good people. But you can learn.

We have to forgive ourselves for the mistakes we've made in relationships and take on the responsibility of learning new skills and unlearning old patterns.

Many of us didn't learn how to love ourselves even when someone stops loving us. Many never learned that a relationship is ultimately meant to feel good in our bodies. Even though a long-term relationship will go through periods of unrest or tension, at the end of the day, a relationship should feel like a safe harbor to come home to.

· ·

PRACTICING THIS TRUTH

Self-Reflection

One of the most powerful questions we can ever ask ourselves is, *How am I contributing to what is not working in my love life?*

In your journal, respond to the following questions:

Could I be more discerning in choosing a partner?

What does it look like when I'm reactive in my relationships?

How have I tolerated mistreatment from others?

How have I struggled to see that I'm worth the love that I desire?

What do I struggle to communicate?

How have I avoided hard conversations?

Remember Jennifer? One of her biggest challenges in a relationship was that she was highly reactive. Whenever she felt insecure, instead of taking a moment to collect her intense emotions, she would immediately react and pick fights with her partners. Part of our work together was to teach her how to stretch the time between being activated by something and responding to it. This is not an overnight process. It is a practice. She had to consistently practice noticing what was happening inside her body when she felt threatened. Then she had to practice taking a few minutes to breathe and question her thoughts, and then respond instead of lashing out. This took patience, diligence, and lots and lots of practice. In Truth 6, I will write more about training ourselves to be less reactive.

As I said earlier in this chapter, we have to be the change we wish to see in our love lives, and it begins with us. Personal responsibility is the only way to create change. A big part of personal responsibility lies in how we care for ourselves.

True Self-Care

A healthy relationship demands that we nurture the relationship we have with ourselves. In order to effectively take care of ourselves, we have to understand our nature. If you consider yourself to be sensitive (meaning you are deeply attuned to your environment and to the emotions of others, or you easily become overwhelmed with too much mental or physical stimulation), a giver (meaning you are quick to help and love to nurture), or both, then you often need some extra help prioritizing yourself. What I am about to write will be particularly useful to you.

Being highly sensitive is not a character flaw. It is your nature.

Being a giver means you value generosity and you derive joy from giving to others. It is not a flaw.

Rejecting your own high sensitivity will force you into a war with yourself. You must honor this part of you, while also taking measures to balance your mind and body to be more resilient.

What follows are suggestions I give to all my clients. These are especially crucial if you are sensitive or working through trauma, or if you tend to overthink or struggle with personal boundaries. Being highly sensitive means that you likely get overwhelmed easily and feel at the mercy of other people's energy and moods. Taking charge of our lives means we commit to practices that we need in order to function better.

Movement

Every day, you must move your body in a way that gives you more energy, not less.

These are the movement practices that I recommend the most to anyone who wants to feel more balanced between their body and mind: long walks, yoga, Pilates, weight training, swimming, and dancing. Nothing gets us out of our heads and into our bodies faster than dancing to music we love.

If playing sports is your thing, that's also a great way to take care of yourself. Sometimes moving your body in a group activity, such as playing tennis or a team sport, can be incredibly useful, because you're meeting your need for connection and community while also moving your body.

If it's possible to do any of these activities outdoors, all the better. If that's not available to you, be sure to spend more time outdoors.

If you're in a relationship, going on a walk together is incredibly coregulating. Working out can be a fun activity to do together.

Play

Play is the most underrated path toward a healthy relationship with ourselves and others, even though play is what makes us feel most alive. And that's what most relationships need more of—aliveness. Most people struggle with being childish in their relationships by being selfish, reactive, unreliable, and inflexible. Being childlike, however, is what heals us. To be childlike is to be open, curious, adventurous, silly, and whimsical. Much of our inner work is actually learning how to return to the more playful, adventurous, creative parts of ourselves, unburdened by all the rules and expectations we live by. Play is what gets us out of our heads and into the present moment. Play is what helps us laugh, and laughter is incredibly bonding.

Do more of what is fun to you. Spend more quality time with friends. Play sports every week, if you like sports. Play Twister with your partner if you're in a relationship. Go on an adventure together or alone. Don't be afraid to be a little silly sometimes—whether that's sending a GIF to your partner or playing board games, if that's your thing.

If you're in a relationship, hug more. Hold hands. Touch is very calming for our nervous systems.

Rest

Every day, you must make time to rest. Resting can look like taking twenty minutes to lie down or just sit and zone out. Resting could mean setting aside one day a week when you have no plans. Meditation is the highest form of rest. There are many different kinds of meditation, and I suggest you find the one that works best for you. The best way to start is to google "guided meditation" and find someone who has a soothing voice that you can listen to for ten to twenty minutes, twice a day if possible. It will be a game changer for your stress and overwhelm.

It takes incredible courage to look deep inside ourselves. This is not just about taking responsibility for our lives; it's about reaching deep inside to find the will and the determination and the inspiration to make the changes that we need to make. Not a lot of people are willing to do this work, because they're too afraid of what they might find. They're also busy blaming everyone else. I want you to know that I see you. The fact that you want to grow, take your love life by the reins, and steer it in the right direction—that is extraordinary. The profound truth of "It Begins with You" is that you have more influence over your love life than you could possibly imagine. Even in your weakest moments, you have the power to heal.

The Mind Is a Battlefield

Stay in your head, and your relationship is dead.

Relationships suffer when we get stuck in our heads, not communicating, creating stories that have little basis in reality. When we feel insecure, doubtful, or uncertain of someone's feelings for us, we can easily (and neurotically) imagine what they're thinking and feeling—even though we actually have no idea what they're thinking or feeling. But the more we convince ourselves that we *know* what the other person is thinking and feeling, the easier it is for *us* to feel rejected, frustrated, angry, and hurt. The more rejected, frustrated, angry, and hurt we feel, the more likely we are to act out, lash out, punish, withhold, cling, project, instigate, and sabotage.

Our minds become battlefields, and we're the only ones who can stop the fight.

If They Really Loved Me, They Would . . .

Kelly, a self-proclaimed control freak, was frustrated with her laid-back husband, Mike. When she came to me, one of the first things she told me was "My husband doesn't validate my feelings." When someone says to me with so much certainty that their spouse doesn't validate their feelings, I know that I'm dealing with a dire situation. This is something that could lead to divorce or, if not, could mean two people staying together who feel unseen, unheard, and miserable.

"What do you mean?" I asked her.

"I have so much to do," Kelly said. She was wearing a beautiful cashmere sweater, with her long brown hair pulled back in a neat ponytail. "I'm overwhelmed most days, and last weekend I had to organize everything for our son's fifth birthday party. Mike kept telling me to relax. He just never understands when I tell him I'm stressed and overwhelmed and—God, he just reminds me of what my fucking father was like with my mom."

Clearly, she was very frustrated.

"I feel like he doesn't validate how I feel. I don't know if my needs are being met." Her tone was laced with resentment.

I probed further. "If he's not meeting your needs, what does that mean?"

She paused, searching for the right words. "I guess it means that he doesn't understand me." Kelly started to tear up.

"And that makes you feel . . . ?" I asked.

"Like he doesn't really see me. That he doesn't care," she said quietly.

"And if he doesn't care, that means . . . ?" I asked gently.

"That . . . that he doesn't love me. That I don't matter like I used to." Tears streamed down Kelly's cheeks as her sadness replaced her rage.

For months, Kelly had been telling herself that Mike didn't truly love her anymore because he didn't seem to care that she was stressed and overwhelmed. Because he didn't console her out of her anxiety, she concluded that not only did he not care about her, but he also wasn't able to fully meet her needs. *He doesn't validate my feelings; he doesn't care; he doesn't get me* became the incantations that would hypnotize her into questioning her marriage.

"Tell me why you're so stressed, Kelly."

"I just feel like I have so much to do all the goddamn time. I work part-time as a personal chef, I'm training to run a marathon, and I run school events with a small group of other mothers at my son's school. Now I know I can be a bit of a control freak, and I'm working on that. I really am. I started doing yoga, and I'm just trying to not be so worried all the time if things aren't running perfectly smoothly." She let out a big sigh.

She sounded like so many of the New York mothers I knew, whom I would often look at in awe: *How do you fit all this in a day and still look good?*

"Wow. You do *a lot*, Kelly. I'm glad you're working on letting go a little. Needing to control everything all the time is very exhausting."

"It is," she said, sounding slightly defeated.

Kelly's was the voice of countless women—especially mothers—who feel they have to be superwomen. Not only do they have to do it all, but they have to do it all perfectly. They feel they need to excel in everything they do—motherhood, relationships, work, maintaining their bodies, and hobbies—and they just keep filling their plates with more tasks and responsibilities. Then, as soon as they sense that they've taken on more than they can handle, they panic and ultimately feel inadequate. They feel like failures. Although I'm not a mother, I know this overwhelm intimately, and I've worked with hundreds of women who know it, too.

"So it's the day of your son's fifth birthday. You said you were feeling extra stressed and unsupported by Mike. Did you say anything to him? How did you react?" I asked.

"Ugh, I got so annoyed at him! I guess it's my tone—like, he definitely knew I was pissed at him."

"I bet that was stressful for him," I said, gently.

She looked taken aback. "Oh. I hadn't thought of that," she answered honestly.

I kept going. "Do you think it's possible that Mike actually does care a lot and the two of you are just caught in a pattern where you're both reacting to each other?"

"Mike is very laid-back and I am type A."

"Right," I said. "So maybe, during your son's birthday party, you both felt overwhelmed by each other's MO, if you will."

I paused to gauge Kelly's reaction. It was very important to me that she felt heard, but it was also my job to see whether I could help them save their marriage. I had little doubt that Mike could have been more attentive to Kelly's needs during their son's birthday party. I was almost certain, however, that Mike was not being inattentive because he didn't love Kelly. Instead, what was happening was that her need to control everything—specifically on that day—overwhelmed him to the point where he felt powerless. He then shut down as a way to protect himself from Kelly's stress.

Kelly told herself a different story: Mike didn't support her when she was overwhelmed and feeling out of control. This meant that he didn't care about her, their marriage, or their love. She had fallen prey to the belief that *if he really loved me, he would* _____. Kelly's mind had become a battlefield, and I needed to help her see things differently so she could reach peace with her husband.

"Does Mike know that you feel worried and sad that he may not love you the way he used to?" I asked. "Or does he just know that you find him annoyingly unhelpful?" I winked with a little smile, hoping she would still feel supported by me even as I challenged her.

She covered her face with her hands. "*Ugh*. I don't know. I suppose I can be a bit hard on him. But sometimes I get more stressed because he's not being helpful when I need him!"

"I hear you, Kelly. I really do. Our inner voice has tremendous influence over our relationships. And if we don't question the voice in our head, it has the power to destroy a relationship. You're so in your head about Mike's intentions that you assume that he doesn't even *care* about you, instead of considering how your stress might be impacting him. You're trying to read his mind. And instead of seeing your role in a pattern you both need to communicate about, you're resentful, Kelly. We both know now that underneath your resentment is a lot of fear and hurt, but regardless, you've built so much resistance toward your husband that you're trapped in a narrative that makes him a careless villain who doesn't love you. And my strong guess is that there is more to this story."

The hard truth is that most relationship problems (including problems in the relationship you have with yourself) stem from negative thoughts and stories. When it comes to our relationship with ourselves, the greatest battle we face is with our own critical minds, which try to convince us we're unworthy. When a couple can't stop fighting, they're not fighting each other—they're in combat with the stories they have about each other.

Kelly, for example, felt unsupported by Mike, and I had no doubt that Mike could've done a better job of acknowledging his wife's overwhelm. That said, Kelly had created a compelling story based on some facts but embellished by a fearful mind that told her Mike was an uncaring, selfish, and aloof husband, just as her father was to her mother. Kelly's story was also missing one crucial piece of information: Mike's experience.

Kelly followed my advice to have a conversation with Mike with a clear four-part intention:

- Listen to his side of the story (active listening).

- Communicate how afraid she was that he didn't love her (vulnerability).

- Share how sorry she was for creating a story that made him out to be a bad husband (responsibility).

- And state what she needed to feel more supported during times of overwhelm (clear expression of needs).

What she uncovered from that conversation was illuminating. Kelly was often stressed-out (a problem she was well aware of and was working on) but didn't realize the impact her stress was having on Mike. Instead of preemptively asking for extra support, she got in her head, where her mind became a battlefield of assumptions about Mike's feelings. She would then lash out and complain when she didn't get what she needed, while her husband, overwhelmed by her chaotic and controlling energy, felt powerless and withdrew.

After just one radically honest conversation, Kelly could finally let go of the story that Mike was uncaring and unsupportive of her needs. Through our work together, she learned how to stop trying to be a superwoman and instead learn healthy habits for managing stress and better ways to communicate with her husband about what she needed, instead of resenting him for not reading her mind.

If we don't discipline our minds, we can easily fail to see the person we love. Instead, we'll see our mother, or our father, or an ex. If we want to have healthier relationships, our task is to challenge ourselves to question some of our narratives about the other person and, instead, communicate. Because if we don't, we'll build up a whole lot of mental and physical resistance against our partner. This resistance leads to resentment, and the more resentful we become, the more closed off we become. The more closed off we are, the more connection fades, and the more connection fades, the quicker we are to overreact and blame. This is how couples' negative stories about each other get out of control, and this is why many relationships end.

Thankfully, winning the battle is not as complicated as you might think. The mere acknowledgment that we might be stuck in our heads and lost in a story that is fueled by fear is by itself a huge step in the right direction. When we admit that our minds may have gotten the best of us, we can tame our fear and make room for the better part of our minds—the part that is open to seeing things differently—to take over. This is definitely an evolved relationship skill that I believe everyone is capable of, but it does require responsibility. We must be responsible for communicating so that we don't get resentful. If we refuse, we'll keep fighting with our partner and break up. Or we'll stay in the relationship and be miserable.

Then there's the utter devastation you experience when someone you love breaks your heart. Sometimes, the person you love can't show up for you at the level that you need them to because they're too caught up in problems, stress, and feelings of unworthiness that have nothing to do with you. Sometimes the person you love wants something different from what you want out of life. When this happens, too many of us will berate ourselves that if only we had been more loving, more beautiful, more important, the other person would have forgotten all their problems and chosen us. Instead of recognizing that the person we love needed to help themselves before they could be in a relationship, we tell ourselves a fiction: that they left because we're not enough for them to stay. That is the lie that destroys our lives.

Change Your Story, Change Your Life

Inside our minds lives an untamed, restless monkey that swings from one fearful, critical thought to the next.

Monkey mind is a Buddhist concept that describes a mental state of lack of control of one's thoughts—restlessness. It's suffering. Yoga is about understanding the mind and learning how to train and tame the monkey inside of us so that our minds can be clearer, more focused, and connected to our hearts.

When we get trapped in our monkey minds, we feel uncertain, anxious, and—in Kelly's case—frustrated and resentful. Because the monkey mind is unruly and chaotic, it can easily become a destructive force in our lives that can gravely affect our mental health, prevent us from moving on from a breakup, and sabotage a relationship. It is a well-known life skill to be able to calm our minds, but I believe the most underrated relationship skill is the ability to question our thoughts so that our monkey minds don't take over our relationships.

I'm someone who's definitely had to put in the work to tame her monkey mind. I have an overactive mind, which has worked very well for me creatively and professionally, but which can easily—without mindfulness and diligent practice—cause me great suffering. Overthinking can sometimes take over my life. I feel particularly empathetic and compassionate toward people who struggle with this problem, because I understand this part of the mind so well. I've spent the past twenty-five years of my life studying the power of the mind, and I also know from my own experience how easy it is to get caught in the middle of a battlefield where the monkey is the general.

Yes, some people struggle with overthinking more than others do. But everyone knows what it's like to get trapped in their thoughts. And as Wayne Dyer says, "Change your thoughts, change your life."

I would add to that thought: change your story, change your life.

I think one of the most difficult experiences to go through in life is a breakup or a divorce. There are very few things in life that will trap us in our heads as much as the pain of having to let go and move on from a relationship that has ended. Not every breakup is the same, but certain breakups are emotional catastrophes that bring us to our knees and make us question our very existence. And it's been my experience, professionally and personally, that when people go through a very painful breakup, the story we tell ourselves about the breakup determines how we survive it.

Everyone goes through different stages in heartbreak, like stages of grief, beginning with an acute phase, which can feel like withdrawal from a drug. You feel like you've lost the most important person in your life; for some people, it feels as if they've lost a limb. One of the most painful things is to feel as though someone has died when *they're actually still alive.* In this acute stage, people go through an identity crisis because they're no longer someone's spouse, partner, boyfriend, or girlfriend. They're now single.

When we're in a relationship with someone, our nervous systems are synchronized. We're in sync. A breakup is such a disruption to the natural order of your life—the flow of your days, your daily habits, your social life. It's such a huge shock to the system that the acute phase is devastation. During the acute stage, there's a tremendous amount of anxiety, a loss of appetite, an inability to sleep, and a feeling of being emotionally out of control.

You are in survival mode. Because when you lose love, it feels as if you are going to die.

I think everyone knows how messy our minds are when we go through a breakup. We are questioning everything. If we believe in God, we're questioning God's existence. We're questioning our ability to survive. We're replaying certain conversations over and over in our heads. We feel we have no control over our minds; they become totally obsessive. We are questioning our decisions, our behavior, our worth.

One minute you're aching for your ex and feeling like your limb is missing, the next minute you're hating them. When you're going through a breakup, you will feel as if you've lost your mind. It's almost as though you've been possessed.

To feel like a slave to your own thoughts and emotions is suffering. And that's the enormity of heartbreak.

Even though everyone's timeline is different and depends on the relationship, how things ended, and a person's support system, usually after six months, people start to feel a little bit better. After a year, people generally start to feel more like themselves again.

But some people get stuck in telling the story of their pain and struggle to move on. That was Sarah.

When I met Sarah, it had been eight months since her boyfriend of three years broke up with her when she returned from a vacation with her girlfriends. She was thirty-nine years old, an intelligent, intuitive, emotional person who felt things very deeply. She was a sensitive empath who believed in manifestation and loved reading Eckhart Tolle books.

But she was also very stuck.

During our first session together, she told me her breakup story.

"I feel like I lost my best friend. We were so close. I don't know how we got here."

"What happened? In your view, why did you break up?"

"For the last year, we didn't get along that well. We would get into these really big arguments. I have abandonment issues because of my father. He was never around when I was a kid. So every time we got into a fight, I would then get really, really anxious, and then I'd feel kind of clingy. I was in therapy. He was in therapy. We did therapy together, and it helped a little bit, but we just couldn't seem to reach common ground."

"What were you fighting about?"

"We first met when I was thirty-five and he was thirty-seven. I wasn't really sure that I wanted kids, and he wasn't sure either. So we put it on the back burner. But two years into our relationship, I was thirty-seven, and I started to think, *Wow, maybe I do want kids.* And when I brought it up to him, he was like, *I don't think I want kids.* And that's when things started to get weird between us. We would have discussions about it. He would say that he *loved* me, but he didn't want to have a *family* with me—but if he loved me, wouldn't he want to have a family with me?"

Sarah was fighting back tears as she raced through her words. I told her to put one hand on her heart and take some slow deep breaths, focusing on the exhale, so that she could connect to her body more.

"That's really difficult," I said to her. "When one person wants kids and the other person doesn't, that's a really big deal."

She nodded. "Yeah, it is. I even tried to talk myself out of wanting a baby."

"So how did you handle that? I'm assuming this is what led to you breaking up?" I asked.

"It was a year of going back and forth. I was feeling really resentful toward him for not wanting to have a baby with me. I think there were times when he was frustrated with me for trying to change his mind. We were starting to get on each other's nerves, so I thought it would be a good idea to take a little time-out and go on a girls' trip. He had a lot of work to do. I went away for a long weekend with my friends. When I came back, he said, 'It's over.'"

"Just like that? You walked in, and he said, 'It's over'? There was no conversation?"

"Yeah, he basically said, 'It's over,' and I said, 'What are you talking about?' We sat down and talked. He said he doesn't want to stand in the way of me having a family. He feels like he's had so much pressure on him, and he's been very clear he doesn't want kids. His mind for now is not going to change, and he doesn't want to get in the way of me having what I want. And I told him I want him *and* I want the family!"

As she was telling me the story, I felt particularly affected. My ex-husband really wanted a child, and I did, too, but because of a really difficult miscarriage, I questioned whether that was going to be possible for us. To have kids or to not have kids became the focal point of our relationship and ultimately broke us apart. I am acutely aware of how crucial it is to be on the same page about kids, in order to make a relationship work, and equally how incredibly painful it is not to be entirely on the same page and consequently to have to end things. I felt an enormous amount of compassion for her in that experience.

"It was just so unfair," Sarah said, "the way that he broke up with me. I feel so betrayed by him. How could you do that to someone you love?"

When I heard "betrayed," my ears perked up. It occurred to me that perhaps what was keeping her stuck—unable to let go eight months later—was that she believed she had been betrayed.

A pivotal moment in my heartbreak recovery was when I realized that what was holding me back from truly moving on had very little to do with my ex-husband.

Instead, it was the belief that I wasn't worth the love, that I didn't mean much to him, because of the way he decided to end the relationship: through a text that he wasn't coming home, followed by a phone call—while my mom was dying of lung cancer.

This is what I see every single time with people who are stuck in the intense grieving stage, even after a lot of time has passed and a lot of processing has occurred. At some point, it's not about them. It has more to do with the story we tell ourselves, which calls into question our significance and value. What was once the mourning of a relationship is replaced with a belief that we are inadequate—a belief that makes moving on extremely difficult.

But here's the truth: we can love each other and mean a lot to each other and still break each other's hearts.

Breaking up is very challenging for everyone, because relationships rarely end because of a lack of love. They more commonly end because of irreconcilable differences.

I wanted to help Sarah change the betrayal narrative she was telling herself.

I asked her, "Were you happy? It sounds like you were fighting a lot, knowing you wanted kids, but he didn't. That sounds very stressful. Sometimes when we're grieving a relationship, we will have amnesia and forget how stressed-out and unhappy we were leading up to the breakup."

She paused to reflect. And then she let out a sigh. "The last year was very hard. We did not get along."

"Sarah, I know what it's like to go to bed every night with your significant other, without getting along. And having to face the very harsh reality that you want very different things in life and not feeling like you can reach the solution. I can only imagine how unhappy you were."

Sarah started to tear up.

I continued, "The two of you were facing a mountain that felt unscalable. It's a really common mountain that a lot of couples have to face and decide whether they're going to climb it together. The fact that the two of you didn't figure out how to climb it is okay. It's part of life. When I listen to your story, it sounds to me like the two of you really tried the best that you could—*because* there was so much love there. My guess is that his decision to end things was a very difficult decision to make, and he did it to put an end to the misery that the two of you were facing."

As I continued to work with Sarah, my goal was to help her move on, and the only way for her to move on was for her to see the breakup from a different perspective, so that she could finally have freedom to focus on herself.

When a relationship is not working, with two people trying to maneuver through irreconcilable differences, it takes up so much mental real estate and energy. One of the hardest lessons we will ever have is learning to accept when someone's part in our story is over. It's a very difficult thing to move on from someone you love, even when the reason to break up and move on is very clear and valid.

What was making it almost impossible for Sarah to move on was that she was not seeing things clearly. She was stuck on this one detail of the story: *How could he have broken up with me that way?*

My job was to get a clearer understanding of their relationship and to remind her that they'd been breaking up for a year.

"If he hadn't broken up with you," I asked her, "would you still be with him?"

"Probably, because I'm always the one to stay. I have a pattern of staying in relationships past their expiration date. It's hard for me to let go."

"Welcome to the club," I said with a wink, and she laughed.

"But Sarah, if you stayed, then you would be forty and still childless."

"But I could still be childless even now! Single!"

"But at least now there's at least some possibility you can still have a child. Maybe, just maybe, he actually did you a favor," I said gently. "I wish he had done it with more tact. I wish you didn't have to come back from a vacation to this. And if he was here, I'd tell him he shouldn't have done that. What if letting you go was actually what he felt was the only option and the right thing to do? So that he would no longer stand in the way of what you really want."

"Yes," Sarah admitted, "he told me something like that, too."

"It doesn't make it any less sad, Sarah. Breaking up is hard and sad for everyone. But the true story is that he didn't just break up with you because he doesn't care about you. I think he did what the two of you both knew deep down in your hearts was the right thing to do. Often, there's really no 'right' way to break up with someone, especially after a year of fighting."

Sarah had come to me in a trance, hypnotized by a story her mind was fixated on, about how her boyfriend betrayed her and didn't love her. I helped her to wake up to the truth of what happened between the two of them and to see that her destiny was not tied to the person who left her. And I promised her that in time, she would see why.

At forty-two, Sarah is now married, and she recently had a baby.

. . . .

PRACTICING THIS TRUTH

To have healthier relationships, you must commit to the practice of getting out of your head.

These are specific steps you can take to reframe your thinking when you are caught in a storm of negative thoughts about your partner, date, or yourself, so you can get out of your head more often.

1. **Awareness:** Practice paying attention to when you are ruminating, obsessing, or saying negative things about your partner. You can observe, *I'm in my head right now. I'm caught in a story and maybe I need to take a moment.* You learn how to bear witness by practicing paying attention. When we're in our heads, there are likely very specific physical symptoms that we can pay better attention to: tight jaw, tight neck and shoulders, shallow breathing, and tension in the facial features, especially around the eyes and between the eyebrows. Noticing those physical symptoms can help us become aware. Awareness is about training ourselves to get better at recognizing when we're ruminating due to stress. Recognizing when we're in our heads can help us avoid getting

seduced by a negative story that could potentially sabotage our happiness.

2. **Pause:** You want to interrupt the story. That's when you take a moment to pause, take a deep breath in, and take a deep breath out. When you're caught in the story, there's a lot of physical and mental tension. Pausing is actively taking a moment to breathe and release some of the tension. You're using your breathing to slow down your thinking; when we are caught in a story, we tend to be thinking fast. Our thoughts tend to be somewhat circular. And so we just want to slow down.

3. **Calling trusted counsel:** Whether this is a trusted friend, family member, or therapist, you want to call this person and say, "The story I'm telling myself is _____." You're not looking for someone to vent at; you want to speak to someone who can be a voice of reason and help you see whether your mind is a battlefield right now. When our minds become a battlefield, we lose reason. We need someone who isn't in our minds, who can bring us to reality and say, "Perhaps you are overreacting." That person can offer perspective. Sometimes talking to trusted counsel is a way to get out of our heads.

4. **Exercise and movement:** This is a profound way to get out of our heads in general. Exercise is very helpful for rumination. A long walk can be helpful, too. Refer back to Truth 1 for more movement practices.

5. **Focus and inquiry:** When we're stressed about our relationship—whether it's a new one or one we've been in for years—it's easy

to get in our heads and become edgy, irritable, and fearful. We become divorced from the wisdom of our hearts, intuition, *and* rational thinking. When this happens, we unintentionally become individualistic, selfish, and self-obsessed. Instead of equally caring about *our partner's* needs, or the needs of the relationship, we become obsessed with *our* needs and whether or not they're being met by our partner. Instead of appreciating everything our partner has to offer us and the world, we'll focus on their flaws and fixate on everything that is wrong about them. Instead of giving a new date a chance, we hypervigilantly look for red flags. You can ask yourself a series of questions when you're in the middle of this battlefield: *What am I focusing on? What else could this mean? Is it possible I'm not seeing this clearly right now? Could there be more to the story? Could it be that I'm in a bad mood or stressed-out, and I'm not seeing things clearly?* These are very powerful questions.

6. **Connecting to our heart's intelligence and intuition:** Connecting to your heart is about seeing the person you love as who they are, rather than a monster. It also means connecting with your body when you're dating: Do you feel good when you're around this person? Could it be that you're stressing out about old stuff from the past? What feels good in your body right now?

If You're Dating

Dating can send us into a tailspin of overanalyzing and feeling inadequate. How many times have you been on a date that you thought went well, only to later dissect the conversation and conclude that you didn't come across as cool, smart, or interesting? How many times have you played an entire movie in your head about what someone is doing, thinking, and feeling while leaving your text on read?

You need to get out of your head and into your body. Ask yourself: *How do I feel when I'm with this person? Do I actually really like this person, or am I consumed with getting them to like me?*

Tools for When You Can't Stop Replaying the Same Thoughts

Journaling: I recommend this first thing in the morning, to get everything in your mind on the page. You are not looking for coherent sentences, grammar, or spelling. You're not going to read it again. It's just a brain dump.

Speaking to trusted counsel: Talking to (not venting at) someone else, such as a coach, a therapist, or a mentor can help you gain perspective.

Giving back: When we are all in our heads, one of the fastest ways to get out, besides exercise, is to help someone else. Whether that's volunteering or helping someone with a big problem, service is a way for us to get out of our heads.

Personal Stress

I believe stress isn't talked about enough in terms of its impact on relationships.

Stress is an emotional and physiological state in which we feel uncertain and out of control. When we are stressed-out, we feel ill-equipped to meet the daily demands of our lives, and many people will lose their motivation to contribute to a partner and a relationship.

Stress is a part of life. There will be seasons of life when extremely difficult challenges arise, and it's normal to experience prolonged stress during these times. All of us have trauma. All of us have pressure. Not only do we live in stressful times, but we're all trying to meet the demands of achieving at work, excelling in parenting, accomplishing as lovers, and more. But we must build awareness about how our stress impacts a romantic relationship. Do you constantly vent to your partner? Do you get controlling? Do you stop being present? Do you stop wanting sex? Do you snap? Do you shut down? Do you become needy? Do you stop having fun?

When we're stressed-out, we cannot see clearly. We just can't trust how we see ourselves, life, or our circumstances when we're stressed. We will get in our heads much more in this state, concoct the worst-case scenarios, and become closed off from seeing what is good. And unfortunately, people think that when their lives get less stressful, their relationships will improve. This isn't true. The truth is that their relationships will improve when they change the way they react to stress.

To let go and reduce stress, I recommend:

Daily meditation.

Yoga nidra can be incredible for stress reduction. It's the practice of deep relaxation, guided by a teacher, as you lie down in a very comfortable position. It's a form of meditation in which you slowly and incrementally release tension in your body, so you can go into a deep state of relaxation. There are short videos available for free on YouTube.

Daily movement, even if it's just a long walk.

Removing some things from your plate.

Periods of white space throughout the day (to walk or sit down on the couch and be quiet without looking at your phone).

Creativity (painting, drawing, singing—any hobby that feels good to you is incredibly stress-reducing).

Spending time with a pet.

Spending time with a good friend and coregulating your nervous system.

Giving back.

So many relationship problems are caused by people creating fiction in their minds about their partner. Couple that with a lack of communication, and what you have is a recipe for relationship chaos. We don't talk enough about how our thinking plays a huge role in the health of a relationship. A story in our head has the power to completely destroy a relationship—or transform it.

Lust Is Not the Same Thing as Love

You meet someone. You feel an immediate surge in energy—a spark of electricity that feels as though it's lighting up your insides. You start dating, and the time you spend together feels profound. You have deep, long conversations about the meaning of life and share intimate details about your pasts with each other. Your physical connection is off-the-charts electric. For the first time in what maybe feels like a long time, you feel seen, desired, and relaxed in a lover's company. *Finally*, you think, *I've found "The One."*

But as the weeks pass, you can't help but notice that you're not spending as much time together as you did at the beginning. You feel *so good* when you're around them, but when you're apart, you feel unsettled, insecure, and aching to feel connected once more. They don't text as much as they did in the very beginning. Instead of knowing exactly when you're going to see them again, the way you did in the beginning, it's now unclear and left until the last minute, and when you *do* hang out, something feels off. When you try to broach the subject of feeling less connected to this person, they seem annoyed and uninterested in having a conversation about it. Something has changed. This "amazing" person doesn't seem as enamored by you anymore, and you don't know how to make sense of it. The truth is, you're heartbroken. Even though you've only been seeing them for about a month, your connection with this person felt stronger than any connection you have had in a really long time, and you saw a future with them. You love them. Or do you?

The truth is, some people are ready for a connection, not a relationship.

Connection Is Overrated

At forty-nine, Danielle was a successful businesswoman. She ran two charities, had a teenage daughter, and had been divorced for six years. She was smart, self-aware, good-looking, kind, and funny. Since her divorce, she'd had one emotionally draining two-year relationship with someone who routinely pulled away and struggled to meet her needs. She came to me ready to start over and fall in love again.

Danielle is someone we in the coaching world would call "coachable," which means she was ready to hear the truth and take direction from me.

When she met Justin, a successful and kindhearted divorcé, on a dating app, they immediately hit it off. After a couple of great weeks of seeing each other regularly, Danielle was elated and had already begun to imagine her future with Justin. She couldn't wait to go away together and meet each other's kids and inner circle of friends.

"We have the best time together, Jillian. I feel so comfortable around him and I haven't felt connected to anyone like this in *such* a long time. I *really* like him," she confessed.

I wanted badly to be happy for Danielle. But why wasn't I? I needed the reassurance that her feelings were reciprocated by Justin before I could celebrate with her. I'm fiercely protective of my clients, and my job with singles is to help them make better choices in partners. Given Danielle's past experience of being in a two-year relationship with someone who couldn't meet her needs, I had to be skeptical. I knew I would have to help her get grounded.

And then she said something that was a big red flag.

"The only thing is, he doesn't reach out to me as much and lately he's so busy that trying to make plans with him is really difficult. We had all this momentum in the beginning, but it feels like he dropped the ball. I don't get it."

"Did you ask to see him? You can tell him that you would love to spend more time with him, Danielle."

Turns out, Danielle did try to make more plans with him. He would always respond positively but then complain about how busy he was, and he kept rescheduling their dates.

Danielle was overall a very confident and independent person. But in matters of the heart, she would often compromise her needs. With Justin, she was determined to stick it out to see whether things would change.

I immediately called bullshit on Justin in my head. Too busy to see her? Rescheduling dates?

If a genie in a bottle could grant me one wish, it would be to give me a magic wand that I could use to immediately make people see their worth and not wait around for someone who is basically a stranger to see their worth, too. Justin, for whatever reason, was not investing anymore in getting to know Danielle. If only her sharp business savvy could be applied to her dating life. Danielle was a goddamn catch, and I was going to do everything in my power to help her harness her power instead of giving it away.

"What exactly are you waiting to change? His schedule or . . . *him*?" I asked directly. "I know how much you like him and how strong your connection feels, but right now he's not acting like someone who wants your connection to evolve into a *relationship*. Since you *do* want a relationship, I think it's a good idea to bring this up. Tell him what you've observed, how you feel, and what you want. You've got nothing to lose and everything to gain."

Danielle agreed and followed through with my direction. She discovered her worst fear was true. He wasn't ready for anything beyond their casual dating because he was still recovering from his divorce. Danielle had only known him for six weeks, but she was absolutely heartbroken. She was intoxicated by the chemistry they shared in the beginning and didn't want to face the somber truth that he wasn't who she had projected him to be. He wasn't ready for a relationship, even though she tried to convince herself that he was. I warned Danielle not to continue to see him casually knowing that she wanted and needed much more. I told her that it would only bring her more confusion and pain.

"I know . . . but . . ." she hedged.

I buried my head in my hands. I was so close to helping her make the right choice, and now I could feel her slipping through my fingers. But then I remembered the sage advice given to me by my mentor: "Jillian, just because someone isn't changing fast, it doesn't mean they're not changing. Sometimes they need to learn one more lesson the hard way until they finally draw a line in the sand."

I relaxed. "Danielle, will you do me a favor? Make sure you're sitting comfortably, close your eyes, and take a long, deep breath in, and a long, slow breath out." I could see her doing these things over Zoom. "Now imagine you're dating someone new, and you feel clear about how this man feels about you. You don't have to wonder when he'll call you next, because you know he will. You don't hesitate to call him, because you know he'll answer or call you back as soon as he can because he's excited to connect with you. There's no confusion, no mixed messages, and the relationship has a nice, steady momentum. How does that feel?"

"Incredible."

"Great. You *can* have that. Just not with Justin. And I promise you, he's not the last man on earth."

Chemistry Is What Makes Us Feel Alive

The emotional intensity of lust can feel a lot like love, but it isn't. It's an infatuation with a dream. It's the escape from the fear that we will be alone forever.

It is chemistry.

Feeling wanted feels really good, but being desired is not the same thing as being valued. And for a lot of people, the stronger their desire, the weaker their judgment. When the chemistry is so strong that you lose your mind and throw all your standards and boundaries out the window, you're headed into a storm of unmet needs, insecurity, and self-neglect. I don't know many people who haven't—at least once—completely lost their minds over someone they barely knew or who was completely wrong for them. By losing our minds, I mean we make the other person the center of our universe, plan our future with them (even if just in our mind) and perhaps tolerate crumbs, inconsistency, or even abuse. It could also mean that because of the intense attraction we feel to someone, we try to force what was meant to be a brief romance into a partnership, only to see it crash and burn.

But *why* do we do this? Why is it so easy to be at the mercy of chemistry?

It's simple. Chemistry is what makes us feel alive.

When we can't stop anxiously obsessing about when they're going to call or text, what we're aching for is not actually them. Instead what we're yearning for is a feeling. It's the feeling of being totally alive, unburdened by the boring monotony of our lives and the utter loneliness that comes with being single for longer than we would like to be.

We've been conditioned by movies and literature to believe that love is the same thing as lust. That if we don't feel completely out of our minds, stressed-out, anxious, and manic about someone, then we must not be in love. We're trained to believe that if we don't feel life is meaningless without this person, then it must not be love. We've been brainwashed into associating the roller coaster of a tumultuous relationship with loving someone. The truth is, when we feel ungrounded, anxious, and overly consumed and preoccupied—even if these feelings are not completely interfering with our lives—what we're feeling is lust, not love. To be clear, chemistry is important. I wouldn't get romantically involved with someone I wasn't attracted to, and I certainly don't expect that of you, either. But a relationship demands that we sustain a connection through the months and years of experiencing the vicissitudes of life together. Lust is easy: our body's natural chemicals, such as pheromones, oxytocin, dopamine, and serotonin, do most of the work for us.

Why are we attracted to some people and not others?

This is the million-dollar question.

We will be drawn to people who have physical features that we find attractive and not drawn to those who have physical features we find unattractive. But have you ever been really physically attracted to someone you didn't think was classically good-looking? Or have you ever been so attracted to someone's energy or mind that eventually you became sexually attracted to them?

Chemistry is in many ways a complete mystery. Some theories suggest that pheromones—hormone-like chemicals that are secreted mostly through our skin—are responsible for physical attraction. This makes sense, because it's impossible to be attracted to someone whose smell we don't like, and when we love someone's smell, we're definitely going to be drawn to them.

According to psychological theory, we will be physically attracted to people who register as familiar to our subconscious.

The term "subconscious" was first coined in 1889 by the psychologist Pierre Janet, who hypothesized that, underneath the critical thought of our conscious, awake minds, a strong awareness exists that is the source of our memories of past experiences. Sigmund Freud later argued that the subconscious is the source of human behavior, and while we are aware of what happens in our conscious minds, we are in fact unaware of what goes on in our subconscious. The study and understanding of the subconscious mind is at the core of human psychology.

There's an old saying in the field of psychotherapy: "We marry our father or mother." This can be problematic if you grew up in a troubled household, and you are then attracted to someone who reminds you of the parent with whom you struggled the most. This theory further suggests that our subconscious mind will choose the person who reminds it of the parent we struggle with, in an attempt to reenact painful dynamics from childhood so that we can ideally heal from our trauma. In other words, engaging in a similar dynamic as an adult gives us the opportunity to rewrite our history.

I had a very challenging relationship with my father. My ex-husband's personality could not have been more different from my father's. My ex also looked nothing like my father. But my ex struggled with a mood disorder, and my father was bipolar. My ex-husband would shut down when he was upset, and I would walk on eggshells around him. My father was the king of shutting down, and I always walked on eggshells around him. Is this a coincidence? No, definitely not. But I've also had long-term relationships that did not resemble my childhood at all. In a six-year relationship in my twenties, I never walked on a single eggshell once. I felt loved, supported, and safe.

Why do some of our relationships mimic our childhood trauma, and others don't? Why will we have chemistry with someone who reminds our subconscious of our parent one year, then another year we'll have chemistry with someone totally different? Whoever can concretely figure these things out will probably win the Nobel Prize. What I can tell you is that when you act on chemistry alone, you're acting out of lust. There are many reasons we struggle to distinguish between lust and love and romanticize lust so much. A large piece of that puzzle is composed of the cultural narratives we tell ourselves about what love and relationships look like—specifically the narrative of "The One."

"The One"

When we can't stop thinking about the person we don't really know, what we're aching for is not actually them. It is our *idea* of them—a deeply conditioned ideal of "The One" that we have projected onto them.

It's a craving, not necessarily for the other person, but for magnified, positive emotions—such as bliss, joy, and happiness.

The truth is, "The One" is not a person. It is a metaphor for hope, change, and novelty.

We suffer immensely when we feel disconnected and alone.

When we feel connected, what we're really feeling is a sense of oneness with something or someone else. Disconnection makes us feel fragmented. Connection makes us feel whole. Everyone's unconscious seeks oneness—whether it's through spending time in nature, building community, giving back, listening to our favorite music, moving our bodies, traveling or having an adventure, or connecting with God or the universe.

To feel "at one" with anything, whether it's a higher power, nature, a pet, or another person, is to feel the deepest love imaginable. Think about the times when you felt totally alive, fully in the present moment, and completely content with life, unburdened by stress and endless what-ifs. Maybe it was just a moment when you were at a concert surrounded by thousands of people simultaneously listening to and being moved by your favorite music. Maybe it was during sex with someone you love. Maybe it was that time you went on a hike and, when you finally sat down to rest and look around at the beautiful scenery, you realized how insignificant your problems were. Maybe it was during a great afternoon with a dear friend.

To feel oneness is to feel complete.

"The One" in romantic relationships represents the pure love and wholeness we seek.

The cultural narrative tells us there's one soulmate out there who will complete our life. My interpretation is that "The One" is the person we feel oneness with, and when we first fall in love, that's when we feel that interconnectedness most intensely. This is why it's so damn addictive, even though the story we're told about "The One" falls short.

The Myth of "The One"

No one exists to complete us.

The idea that "The One" is someone who will never disappoint us, love us no matter what, and always make us orgasm, is deeply ingrained into our psyches and is gravely harming our romantic relationships because it sets the wrong expectations.

This myth has convinced us that when we feel insanely attracted to someone we barely know, we must have met "The One."

This myth has also hypnotized us into believing that there is just *one* person who will put back together all the pieces of our fragmented selves and fill in all the gaps of our emotional voids.

The truth is, that incredible feeling of wholeness and aliveness is an emotional state of being that comes from deep within ourselves. That deep, blissful pure love we feel when we're falling in love is simply a reminder of the love and joy we're capable of experiencing. It reveals the love and passion that are already inside of us, waiting to be recognized and awakened, with or without the presence of a romantic partner.

The truth is, there is no singular *One*. There was "The One" who was perfect for you when you were seventeen, and there was "The One" who came into your life when you were twenty-five and ended up teaching you a huge lesson. There was "The One" you ended up marrying and then divorcing.

I was totally convinced that my ex-husband was "The One." I'll never forget our first conversation, standing in the hallway in our sweat-drenched clothes, clutching our yoga mats after class. There was an instant spark between us, generated by our quick, electrifying banter. Wit and banter are my love languages, and this guy didn't skip a beat. After our fifteen-minute conversation, he already knew that I was a first-generation American and that my beloved stepfather had just passed away. He also knew that I was obsessed with this coconut milk you could only get at this one health food store in Manhattan and that my birthday was in a couple of days.

Two days later, on my birthday, he showed up to class with my favorite coconut milk.

That was it. He was "The One."

Our relationship started immediately after our first date the following week. We dove in headfirst and did not take our time. We spoke every day, texted multiple times a day, and had sleepovers multiple times a week. I basically did everything I tell my clients and social media followers not to do. My naive rationale at the time was that at my age, I wasn't inexperienced, and neither was he. I had been in a few serious relationships in my life, and I'd just taken a year off dating after two crappy casual relationships; I was ready for another serious relationship. He had been divorced for two years and had moved on. Plus, with our chemistry, I was convinced nothing was going to stop us.

When I look back at the first few weeks of my relationship with my ex-husband, I can't help but laugh at myself and the situation. Every day, he told me that I was his dream girl, and two weeks in, he said, "I love you." I loved that he would screen all his calls but always answered mine. I loved that he rarely made time in his busy work schedule for anyone except for me and his family. I loved that he introduced me to his parents within just a few weeks, and I loved that I got along famously with both of them. I also loved that he was the first guy I'd met in more than ten years whom I sincerely got along with and had fun with. Ultimately, we love-bombed each other, by which I mean that we were two adults who had no idea how to process our enthusiasm for each other and therefore acted like two teenagers falling in love for the first time.

People often fall in lust with their projected illusions of each other. Mature love says: *I see all of you and I accept all of you.*

The truth is, you ultimately decide who your "one" will be. And when you do decide, you'll have to make that choice many, many times throughout your relationship. My hope is that you choose the one who gives you the support and freedom you need to fully express yourself in the world, so you never have to suppress who you are and pretend to be anyone you are not.

Love isn't just a feeling—it's an intentional practice, a daily ritual, a verb.

What Does It Mean to Love?

I've spent the past ten years helping people understand what it means to truly love someone in a romantic relationship and, thus, what it means to be loved. To make a relationship thrive, we have to understand that love isn't just a feeling. We have to *do* love.

Anyone can fall in love, but to love someone well beyond the honeymoon phase requires another skill set.

Love is a skill that requires mindfulness and self-awareness. Love isn't just a feeling. It's an intentional practice that requires action. To love well means that we have to get over our egos and take ownership of our energy, because a relationship is built and is only as healthy as the two people who are in it.

Love is energy that needs momentum to sustain itself for the long haul, and we are the drivers of that momentum. To love someone is to make a conscious choice to accept someone we often will not understand. It means we love our partner even when they annoy us. It means that we show up as the "right person" and that we don't just expect the other person to be right. It means consistently disciplining our wild minds to keep them from creating stories that make us blame our partners instead of seeing our part also. To love someone involves collaboration, negotiation, resisting the comfort zone, and togetherness as well as distance. In order to love, we have to be compassionate, empathetic, self-aware, and understanding.

To love someone is to love them in the ways that they need us to, not just in the ways that are comfortable for us.

To love someone is to accept their past and commit to not being a continuation of the part of their past that has caused them hurt and suffering.

To love someone is to consistently remind ourselves that the person we claim to love is a gift, not a given.

To love someone is to accept them for who they are. This means we accept all their nuances, quirks, and eccentricities. This is not the same thing as tolerating abusive behavior or dysfunctional patterns (which I write more about in Truth 4); it simply means that when we truly love someone, we don't try to change who they fundamentally are. A lot of people confuse loving someone for who they are with tolerating less than what we all deserve in a relationship. It is not the same. There will be times where you might have to face the difficult decision of leaving a relationship because you cannot accept (nor should you accept) who this person is and the baggage that they carry. You can also decide not to accept someone simply because they are not the right fit for you and you are not the right fit for them.

Loving someone for who they are means that we don't try to change them into being someone who they are not. We don't try to change a scientist into an artist or an artist into a scientist. We don't try to force someone into being an early riser when they've always been honest about the fact that they're not an early riser. Too many people expect perfection from their partners. And the truth is we can't say, *I like you mostly, but if you could only change these three things, then I could really love you.* You can't play that game with yourself or another person.

To accept someone for who they are is to accept their flaws. That doesn't mean that someone gets a pass to treat you disrespectfully. That doesn't mean you won't have to have conversations about how you can better meet each other's needs. It just means that when you choose to love someone, you are consciously choosing their past and their struggles. I realize that some of you reading this may have a history of accepting less than what you deserve, and if that's the case, I want you to raise your standards so that you do expect to be treated well. But the truth remains that most people have so little tolerance for a partner's flaws that they expect perfection—even though, at the end of the day, we're all flawed. And what do we want more than anything else? We want to be accepted for who we are. We want to know that, even though we are not perfect, someone will love us anyway. And if we want that, how can we expect not to give that acceptance to someone else?

That's why it's important to choose wisely. Everyone has a story. Not every story is a match. You can't stay in the relationship and try to change the other person.

Yes, there's always room to grow. And it's a fair expectation of ourselves and of others that we are willing to grow and improve, to the best of our ability. But we also have to be realistic. There are some things we are never going to change in ourselves and never fully heal.

If you knew certain things were never going to change in that person, would you choose them anyway? There is nothing more maddening, more destructive, and more hurtful than being with someone who wants to change you or with someone you want to change.

We have to be able to distinguish between having tolerance for the imperfections we all come with and recognizing what is truly intolerable.

A relationship filled with true love and understanding requires commitment, accountability, intention, patience, communication, creativity, self-awareness, gratitude, and grit. Being in a loving relationship means we will have to apologize frequently and accept apologies. It means forgiveness. Love says, *When you're in pain, I listen.* Staying in love means we bravely address the issues that are causing any misalignments in emotional and sensual intimacy. Staying in love means that we fight and make up, fight for each other, and fight for harmony and peace in the relationship.

A big lesson I've learned about love is that when our partner's needs are more important than our own, we become a resentful martyr in our own relationship, and we can never *do* love in this state. When our needs are consistently more important than the other's, we become selfish, and we are not loving when we are being selfish. Truly loving someone means that meeting the other's needs is as important as meeting our own.

Generally, people need help to be less sacrificial or less selfish in their relationships. If we're truthful with ourselves, most of us would admit we could use a little help being less of both.

When to Say "I Love You"

The "I love you" we say at the beginning of a relationship is not the same "I love you" we say to each other after we've built a strong foundation of trust. This doesn't diminish our love in the beginning. It simply means that love, and the meaning it carries, changes as we grow and as we grow closer to each other.

I can't tell you when it's the right time to say "I love you." But I can tell you that it's not the right time if you haven't had your first argument yet. I can also tell you that the "I love you" you say in the beginning won't be the same "I love you" that you say once you've seen each other at your worst and have been through tough times together. I believe saying the words is important. Regardless of our love language, we need to hear the words "I love you" come out of each other's mouths *at least* sometimes. If you feel it, say it. But remember, love isn't just a feeling—it's a verb.

Choose Character over Charm

Adam was thirty-one years old. As a quintessential wellness freak, he spent his free time in the gym lifting weights, did cold plunges and saunas every morning, and loved to talk about his new smoothie concoctions and why eating paleo is best for optimal health. He was good-looking, wealthy, and educated, and he wanted a serious relationship that would evolve into a marriage with kids. *Ding, ding, ding!* Adam was the guy many of my millennial, heterosexual, single female clients wanted.

He came to me devastated because the woman he loved broke up with him. She was the exact prototype of the woman he always imagined he would end up with: a beautiful, blond social media influencer in the wellness space named Andrea who loved smoothies, lifting weights, and Pilates.

"How long were you together?" I asked.

"Not long, only like two months," he said quietly.

Part of me wanted to shake him. I wanted to say: *You barely know this girl. You can't possibly love her.*

If only that would help. Truth is, *I* had to snap out of it and remember my compassion. I had to connect to him by feeling his pain.

To help Adam, I had to see myself in him. As much as I cringe to remember the times I cried myself to sleep over boys who didn't deserve my tears, these times were exactly what I needed to remember to help Adam. I knew rejection on a cellular level. In fact, after years of working with people, I've learned that rejection runs painfully deep for everyone. Someone basically says to us, "No, it's not you. You're not good enough for me. I don't choose you. I don't choose to build a life with you." We then become obsessed with the fact that we weren't chosen and convinced that we're not good enough to *be* chosen. Thoughts of how we can prove our worth to the other person and win them over hijack our minds.

Adam did what so many of us have done before: he confused chemistry with emotional intimacy. But that confusion didn't lessen the impact of the rejection. A big part of recovering from heartbreak is letting go of the dream of what we hoped a relationship would be and waking up from the wounded trance that has hypnotized us into questioning our worth.

When Adam met Andrea, he did what so many people do when they meet someone they're attracted to: he put her on a pedestal. Adam was insanely attracted to her. Oh, and to top it all off, she claimed she was "looking for her king so she could relax into her divine feminine and they could blissfully create their conscious relationship with each other." Challenge accepted. Adam was going to prove to her he was her king. Basically, Adam was wellness Ken; he thought he had found his wellness Barbie, and the two of them would be an Instagram power couple and make beautiful Instagram-worthy babies together.

"Okay, Ken, so you found your Barbie, right?" I said with a grin to lighten my delivery a bit. I had to say something a bit cheeky to wake Adam up. After just one session, we already had a good rapport. Plus, Adam's superpower was that he wanted to change, and he loved my directness.

"Ha-ha. I guess I see what you mean. Oh! Get this. She actually admitted to me after our second date that before she met me she was going out on dates with different men six days a week so she could get a free fancy meal."

I looked at him, shocked. "Are you kidding me?"

"Nope."

"So you're obsessing over a woman who literally admitted to you that she has a very low character, and all this nonsense about wanting to create a 'conscious relationship' is actually BS. She uses that rhetoric as a way to make herself feel better, when really she just uses men for her own material gain," I said sharply but calmly.

"Wow." He looked as if he'd just woken up from a monthlong nap.

"Tell me what's really important to you, Adam," I asked.

"Family. Being a good person. Love. Working hard," he answered with certainty.

I went straight into teaching mode. "These are your values, Adam.

Our values are what define our character, and the only way you're going to meet that right girl for you is if you prioritize character over your 'type.' She's not Wellness Barbie—she's Shallow Barbie. And either way, Adam, you're not Ken. You're a real person who is looking for a real connection with someone who wants the same things out of life that you do. Stop putting her on a pedestal and instead see the actual person in front of you."

I had to further point out the discrepancy. "Adam, you are someone who values working on himself to become a better person. You can't date women like Andrea anymore because to do so is to violate your own values. And trust me. I understand your pain, Adam. I really do." I clutched my heart as I spoke to him. "I know what it feels like to be incredibly disappointed when a relationship isn't what we thought it would be. But, Adam, when you speak of her, the only thing you mention is how attracted you are to her, and I find it interesting that not once have you mentioned love. Sometimes when we're really attracted to someone, we have a hard time seeing the actual person standing right in front of us. I think you've always known, deep down, that she doesn't have the qualities you're looking for in a future wife and that you ignored some significant red flags."

"Plus," Adam verified, "she likes to go out all the time, and she drinks a lot of alcohol. That is not my vibe."

"There you go."

"Holy crap. This conversation just changed my life," he said, looking stunned.

Adam's main problem was that because he was so attracted to Andrea, he completely ignored the red flags indicating that she was not a good match for him. Instead, he put her on a pedestal.

The moment we put someone on a pedestal, we're doomed. Instead of seeing the actual person, we see the idealized version of who we expect our potential life partner to be. Instead of seeing the real, flawed person in front of us, we see "The One." When we eventually realize that not only are they flawed but they might even be bad for us, we'll be crushed by the weight of our failed expectations, and they'll be crushed by their fall from grace. Everyone loses.

I Don't Want to Be Anyone's Dream Girl

One of my favorite movies is *500 Days of Summer*. In it, the protagonist, Tom, is a lonely guy who lacks meaning in his life. When he meets Summer, a quirky, pixie-like girl who started working with him at his boring job, he's immediately revived. What follows is a perfect portrayal of a dysfunctional relationship as seen through the eyes of the film's dysfunctional protagonist. Tom is sweet, earnest, and totally infatuated with Summer. Throughout most of the film, he desperately tries to be enough for her so she'll choose him. Summer, on the other hand, is depicted as aloof and avoidant because she's never able to fully reciprocate Tom's love. As a spectator, it's easy to be manipulated into believing that Summer is the emotionally unavailable villain. But the truth is that we, the audience, never truly get to know who Summer is. All we see is the Summer that Tom sees: a shell of a woman Tom decided was perfect. She's a woman on top of a pedestal—a projection of Tom's idealized version of femininity. She's a metaphor for hope in a world in which Tom felt completely disconnected from himself and his life's purpose.

Pedestals are for teenagers. They have no place in adult love.

I've been placed on a pedestal many times throughout my life; to be honest, I enjoyed it until the pedestal fell from underneath me. In the past, instead of being authentically myself, I tried to live up to the perfection that was projected onto me until I just couldn't keep up the illusion anymore. When it didn't work out, I always felt misunderstood. The idea that no one ever loved me for who I am became a central theme of my story. Today, I have no interest in being someone's dream girl, the way I was for my ex-husband. I'm not interested in playing a part in someone's childhood fantasy of what love should look like. I don't belong on anyone's pedestal, and they don't belong on mine. Every single one of us is flawed, and we do the best that we can with the level of maturity and awareness that we have at any given stage of our lives. Every person you meet has a story, but not every story is a match. Choose wisely.

Building a family, going to bed early, and living a healthy sober lifestyle were paramount to Adam, and he wanted a partner who embodied these values as well. Andrea, on the other hand, disclosed that she used men to get free dinners, didn't want a family (at least not anytime soon), and loved to go out until very late multiple nights a week and drink alcohol. The two of them may have had a great physical connection, but as a couple, they didn't have what it takes to make an emotional connection last over the long term. Their goals and values were vastly different, and they didn't understand that wanting the same things out of life is foundational to a long-term partnership.

Relationships need a foundation of trust and safety to survive. A lesson I learned about love later in life is that trust and emotional safety take time to build. We need a lot of experiences together, a lot of tough conversations, and time to test the level of respect and loyalty we have for each other. The first year of a relationship is fragile because building a sturdy foundation takes time, commitment, and care.

Don't Play House with a Stranger

Adam ignored all the obvious red flags that he and Andrea were mismatched; instead, they took their connection from zero to sixty in minutes, like two horny teenagers. Instead of taking their time to get to know each other, they did something that many people in lust do: they "played house" almost immediately following their first date. Playing house is when we do all the things that couples who are in a more advanced stage of their relationship do. For example, when we transition out of the dating stage and into the committed stage of a relationship, this is when we start to spend more time together. We have sleepovers that may extend over multiple days, we go grocery shopping together, make important decisions together, and make plans for the future together. Ultimately, we integrate our daily lives with each other.

Like so many people I've worked with over the years, Adam and Andrea started acting like a couple when they were practically strangers. They texted multiple times a day, saw each other several nights a week, and spent entire weekends together. Not surprisingly, three weeks into knowing each other, they started fighting. If we don't take our time to really get to know each other and see whether we can build a foundation together, our connection will fall apart before we can even call it a relationship. It's like driving a hundred miles an hour in a sports car the day after we get our driver's license—not a good idea.

Trust me, I know what it's like to get swept away by the lust, hope, and novelty of a new "relationship." I remember the absolute mania that comes with liking someone new and not being able to focus on anything other than that person. It feels as though your entire nervous system has been hijacked. It's thrilling and exciting, until you wake up one morning an anxious wreck who doesn't feel in control of her life anymore.

Playing house with someone we hardly know is our effort to skip over the "getting to know you" stage so that we don't have to live with the uncomfortable uncertainty that is inherently part of dating. Too many people skip the necessary conversations about wants, needs, boundaries, expectations, money, lifestyle, and kids and instead think that if they act like a couple, they're actually a couple. They think (and I've been there, too) that because their "connection" is so strong, they should be in a relationship together. Although having a strong connection is crucial, because it motivates us to learn more about each other, both Danielle and Adam have taught us that it just isn't enough.

If you play house with a stranger, you are attempting to build a house on a weak foundation.

Processing Our Enthusiasm

Don't confuse your intense feelings for what is necessary for a relationship.

Guess what? Eventually the intensity will die down—this is a guarantee. And what we're left with are two flawed people with specific values, goals, traumas, and histories. This is when we find out whether we have what it takes to build a house together.

Initially, it's fun to get carried away with the novelty of a new connection. There's something comforting and sweet about getting butterflies as an adult, just like a fifteen-year-old. The flutter in our belly is a pleasant reminder that we still have a beating pulse—that we are very much alive: raw, vulnerable, and thirsty for passion. As I said earlier in the chapter, it is the aliveness we are in search of. But if we don't then take the time to process our enthusiasm for someone, we're likely to get hurt. Without processing, we'll mistake lust for love and chemistry for emotional intimacy, and we could possibly end up in a very unhealthy relationship. The truth is, most of us will use our intense feelings as an excuse to not ask ourselves important questions.

As adults, we need to examine and question these feelings. If you have a pattern of going from zero to sixty with people and playing house with strangers, then processing these feelings is particularly necessary for you, and it might be useful to enlist the additional help of a therapist or coach.

Going Slow

There are couples who went fast from day one and are now happy, stable, and in love.

They are the exceptions to the rule.

As I said earlier, getting seduced by chemistry and rushing through the uncertain early stages of dating almost always leads to disappointment and heartbreak. The antidote is to go slow. But what does it mean to take it slow?

Going slow means regularly checking in with yourself to see how you're feeling about this person and how you feel about yourself when you're with them. Regular check-ins are very useful when you start to feel uneasy with the uncertainty of not knowing where a connection is going. Of course, you want things to progress between you and someone you like, but that is not the same thing as already planning your future with someone you don't know that well who is on their best behavior.

If you're sensitive and get emotionally attached after you sleep with someone you like, then going slow means you wait until you're committed to each other to have sex. Everyone is entitled to do with their bodies what they want to do, so this is not a moral commentary on sex before monogamy or marriage. We can be sex-positive and still acknowledge that sex complicates feeling; we can easily mistake a passionate night with someone for emotional intimacy. Hard truth: sex—even if it's amazing, passionate sex—doesn't carry the same meaning for everyone. If you cannot separate love and sex, that is a beautiful thing you never need to try to change. This is about understanding your psychology and respecting your vulnerabilities. If you've been hurt in the past, you have to be a protector of your heart and wait to be intimate with someone until it has been clearly communicated that your feelings are reciprocated and your goals for a relationship are the same. This will be a game changer for you.

. . . .

PRACTICING THIS TRUTH

Communicating the Pace

Here are some examples of how to communicate your need for a slower pace.

"I really like you and I'm excited to get to know you more. In the past, I've gone really fast and it never worked out. I would like for us to really take the time to get to know each other before we have sleepovers. What do you think?"

"I'm super attracted to you, but I'm in a place in my life where I only want to have sex with someone I know, who I am committed to."

"I would love to go on that trip with you! I just would prefer that we get to know each other more before we start traveling together."

"As much as a part of me would love to see you multiple times a week, I would prefer to take a slower pace. What do you think?"

Loving Intentionally

On a piece of paper or in a journal, answer these questions as honestly as you can. Take your time.

1. How do you want to love your current or future partner?

2. How do you struggle *to do* love?

3. Can you think of a time in a past relationship where you struggled to accept someone for who they were or expected perfection of them?

How to Process Your Enthusiasm for Someone New in Your Life

Do regular check-ins with yourself. Challenge your feelings by asking yourself these important questions:

1. How do I feel when I'm with them and when I'm *not* with them?

2. Do I like myself when I'm with them?

3. Do I feel comfortable being myself with them? Can I safely express an opinion with them?

4. Do I actually like this person, or am I mostly preoccupied with getting them to like me?

5. Do we share the same core values in life?

6. Do we have the same goals in life in regard to family, children, money, and lifestyle?

7. Have I seen them yet when they were stressed-out? What was that like?

8. When they're stressed, are we still able to remain connected emotionally?

9. Are we compatible? Do we agree on what a great Saturday looks like? Do we like to do a lot of the same things?

10. How are we different? Do these differences add to our relationship or cause issues?

5 Powerful Practices to Help You Ground and Recenter Yourself

1. Continue to spend quality time with your loved ones. When you stay connected to your inner circle, you reinforce the fact that you are already loved and that you have a life that is important to you. Loved ones see the beauty in you that you may be failing to see in yourself.

2. Ask a friend or mentor for help. Ask someone who can be objective to hold you accountable and help ground you in reality when your judgment gets clouded by attraction. For example, you

can ask: "Does this look like my pattern to you, or do they seem like a good match for me?" "Am I getting carried away?"

3. Focus on what's important to you, be it work, a hobby, or another responsibility you have. The more you feel connected to what lights you up, the better. This reminds you that you have a life that someone has to fit into.

4. Breathe. Physiologically, enthusiasm can easily transmute into anxiety. The anxiety leads to obsessing and ruminating. Take some deep, slow breaths through your nose into your lower abdomen, followed by slow, longer exhalations through your nose.

5. Move your body. When you feel consumed by this person you're getting to know, take a walk, run, dance, stretch, lift weights— whatever works for you. The fastest way to get out of our heads is though physical movement.

Never forget this important fact: Everyone is on their best behavior in the beginning. No matter how strongly attracted you are to someone, it's impossible to know whether they're the right person for you until you've seen each other stressed-out and you've had a few arguments. How you're able to stay connected—or not—through hard times is the true test of a relationship.

Looking at Chemistry with a New Lens

Chemistry is mysterious. Lust is what happens when we have chemistry, but *lust is not love.* We have to unlearn some of our ideas about "The One," we have to accept some hard truths about what it means to put someone on a pedestal, and we sometimes need to embrace the slower pace even when we're ready to jump headfirst into something new.

Chemistry is absolutely necessary to have a romantic relationship with someone, but it's not enough to build a long-term partnership. We need someone who's going to be in our corner—someone who will be the best friend we've ever had when things get really hard. Because they will. Life will happen, we will experience losses and setbacks, and we will need someone who has the grit, loyalty, and commitment it takes to do life with us. Don't get me wrong: chemistry is important. Just don't give your heart away to someone because there's chemistry. It's not enough.

Here's a truth I know for sure: You're capable of having chemistry with various people. And most of us will experience the best sex of our lives with the worst person for us. Often, sexual chemistry will be the glue that holds an unhealthy relationship together. But each one of us has a choice: go for the person with whom you feel crappy but have intense sex; or go for the person you're attracted to and also feel secure with, and work together to explore and strengthen your sex life. Feeling safe with someone helps us to let go, and letting go is critical for having a positive sensual experience.

If you have a pattern of consistently falling head over heels for people who aren't good for you, then it's a clue that something needs to be healed and retrained. Often that retraining involves unlearning what you've learned about love from Hollywood (like the *After* franchise, centered around a toxic couple) and popular novels (such as *Fifty Shades of Grey* or *It Ends with Us*). Sometimes it will mean working with a therapist to help you unpack and heal unresolved childhood trauma—particularly if you've been in deeply unhealthy or abusive relationships. Almost always it means learning to value yourself more.

(More on this in Truth 4.) The truth is, as important as attraction is, it's also a sneaky little devil that can trick us into settling. That's when we have to decide that we want more than just a chemical connection. We want to feel emotionally connected, too. We want to feel safe and free to be who we really are.

When we grow, the kind of people we're attracted to evolves, too.

TRUTH
4

You Have to Love Yourself

Every person who struggles to have a healthy relationship also struggles to love themselves.

When I was twenty-eight years old, I met David at my yoga studio. He was thirty-six, handsome, and charismatic. When I asked a friend who knew him what he was like, she said, "Hmm. He's complicated. I'm not sure if he would be a good boyfriend, Jillian." It shocks me now to think I didn't see that as a red flag, but I didn't. *Complicated? Not sure he'd be a good boyfriend? Challenge accepted. It will be different with me.*

Instead of heeding the warning, I saw David as a challenge to prove my value and "get" him. I was attracted to him, and that was all I needed to know that I wanted him to want me. When I first met David, I'd been dating casually for a year, and my previous relationship, which lasted almost six years, was healthy and loving. It ended because it had run its course, and our connection became more of a friendship than one shared between lovers. At twenty-eight, I wanted to get married and start a family. I was "ready." Turns out, I wasn't ready at all.

David and I had instant chemistry. The kind of chemistry that completely hijacks your brain, clouds your vision, and makes you blind to glaring red flags. After our very first date of appetizers and white wine in the Nolita neighborhood, he walked me home. As we stood outside the entrance to my apartment building, he wasted no time and kissed me. It was exactly what I expected—amazing. But then, as we passionately kissed on the street at 12:30 a.m. in front of my old, run-down building, he put his hand down the front of my blouse, reached inside my bra, and felt my breast. I remember thinking, *That's bold for a first date.* I remember feeling uncomfortable about it—but I didn't stop him. That was the first time I ignored my instincts about David.

After our date, we were officially a couple, and for about a month, it was bliss. David was attentive, sweet, and funny, and our physical connection was like nothing I'd ever experienced before.

I'll never forget one lazy Sunday morning when we were chatting in bed with coffee and toast, he confessed to me he had a really bad temper.

"Really?" I asked in disbelief. "I can't even imagine that in you."

"Yup." That was all he said.

Please note: If someone you're dating tells you that they have a bad temper, it is a big red flag. What they're really telling you is that they have no self-control and are unable to regulate their emotions. Additionally, they're basically admitting to the fact that they have big work to do on themselves that they have not yet done. And, most important, that rage will eventually be directed toward you, and it will only be a matter of time before you're in a toxic relationship with someone you'll feel unsafe with. No matter how attracted you are to someone, don't ignore this red flag.

David turned out to be the textbook case of a sleazy toxic guy cloaked in a high-class education, with worldly knowledge and good looks. Shortly after our monthlong honeymoon phase, his rage and manipulation surfaced when he asked if he could move into my three-hundred-square-foot studio apartment.

When we met, he was living in a two-thousand-square-foot prewar apartment on the Upper East Side of Manhattan; later, I discovered he rented the spare room to young female models who were visiting New York to try and "make it." David, an aspiring artist from a family of academics, took pictures of these eighteen-year-old models as a way to make extra money from them. When that gig didn't turn out to be lucrative enough to continue living in an Upper East Side apartment, he decided to move into my apartment, which was the size of a large bathroom. When he made this suggestion, my inner voice was loud and clear: *No.*

When I expressed my hesitancy, he got angry.

"Then clearly you're not as committed to me as you claim to be," he said bitterly.

"That's not true," I quickly replied.

"Yes, it is. You're not all in."

Afraid to lose him, I ignored my wise inner voice.

David's short-lived retail business had gone bankrupt before we met, and because his parents were no longer supporting him financially, he also managed to convince me to get a credit card that he could use. Again, I ignored my loud inner voice, which was telling me to leave him. My self-worth was too low and my fear of losing the connection was too high. That card eventually accrued debt, even though I was responsible with money prior to meeting him. Every time I disagreed with him about anything, he would call me a bitch. He called me a cunt almost every day, spit on me twice, and shoved me once. He would slam doors in my face, and once while we were arguing in the car while he was driving, he became so enraged that he threatened to drive the car into a wall and kill us. He took pictures of me naked, put them in his "portfolio" without my consent, and showed them to various people. When I found this out a year later, I confronted him; he claimed it was his art and therefore he had every right to include it in his portfolio and share it. But make no mistake about it, this relationship brought out the worst in me, too. I read his diary. I searched his computer and found that he spent all day on porn sites. I would engage in fights with him under the guise of "standing up" for myself.

Typically, in very unhealthy relationships, there's an addictive cycle of fighting, followed by making up and regaining closeness, followed by more fighting. The relief from finding closeness again is so overwhelming that it keeps people engaged in the cycle. Because the goal of a relationship is emotional connection and closeness, the person with lowered self-worth can easily trick themselves into believing that those pockets of reconnection are enough to sustain the relationship.

I had never been in an abusive relationship before, so I had no idea how low my self-worth actually was. I entered that relationship thinking I was a confident, strong young woman, but the truth was that I didn't love myself enough to believe I was worth being treated with basic respect. My need to be loved was far more powerful than my self-love. I thought I had a high standard, but as it turned out, it was very low. I abandoned every part of myself in that relationship, and what I consequently experienced was soul-deep pain. I eventually had to come to terms with the fact that I allowed such ugly behavior and that, frankly, I still was in many ways a little girl afraid of her own shadow.

After a year of an emotional roller coaster, our relationship finally ended. I wish I could tell you that I finally stood up for myself and kicked him out of my apartment and life—because truthfully, the only way to stand up for yourself in an abusive relationship is to end it and never look back. Instead, he took the initiative and moved out the day after he lost control and, in a rageful fit, threw my television against the wall. When I look back, my only guess is that he finally managed to scare himself enough to know that he was incapable of being in a relationship.

When he moved out, I was left behind to pick up the broken pieces of my self-esteem. It felt terrible, but that relationship was one of the most significant lessons of my life. I had to look in the mirror and admit to myself that as horrible as David was, I allowed behavior that violated every fabric of my being and intuition. This was extremely humbling. I wasn't the strong, self-assured, have-it-all-together woman I saw myself as, and as many others also saw me—and that was a painful reality to face. I vowed to myself that I would never visit the dark side like that again. And I kept my promise.

Whenever our need for someone's love is stronger than our self-love, we will abandon ourselves in the pursuit of their attention and validation. We'll try to win their love even if it's the wrong love; truthfully, in these cases it usually is the wrong love. The person whose attention we are so hungry for is usually the person who does not deserve our love.

Why Is It Hard to Love Ourselves?

A lot of people understand intellectually that they have value. For example, someone could have confidence at work and think highly of themselves in the workplace, but in romantic relationships, they tolerate way less than what they deserve. That's because having strong self-esteem at work comes from being loved for what you do, not for who you are.

My definition of self-love is self-acceptance.

Why is it hard for us to completely love ourselves? Simple. We know every mistake we have made. We know every judgmental, hateful, and spiteful thought we have ever had; every lie we have ever told; every mean or manipulative thing we have ever done. We grapple with every physical, mental, and emotional flaw we wish we didn't have. We live with who we are and what we do every day, so it is impossible to escape our own judgment. And our judgment is ruthless. Most people are terribly hard on themselves. In fact, I'm often astounded at how hard people are on themselves and how hard *I* used to be on myself. We get so stuck in our heads nitpicking every mistake we make because we have too many rules about how we *should* be, how we *should* look, and how we *should* achieve. This is what we do to our romantic partners as well. Instead of appreciating them, we hold them to an impossible standard and judge them for not being who we think they *should* be.

Do You Need to Love Yourself Before You Get into a Relationship?

Some self-help leaders and influencers tell us that we need to love ourselves before we're ready to be or even capable of being in a relationship. Others tell us that we don't have to love ourselves first, because we learn how to love ourselves *through* relationships.

In my view, both theories are true.

You do not have to completely love yourself to be in a relationship. You don't have to live in a cave, single, working on yourself tirelessly to be in a fulfilling relationship. Because—even if you wake up one morning and think to yourself, *I'm healed! I love myself! I can be alone!*—I can guarantee that once you *are* in a relationship, you'll be challenged. The perfectly independent self-loving version of you when you were single will at times feel like a distant memory. That being said, you better believe that if you've ever tolerated crumbs, chased love from unavailable people, or worst of all been in an abusive relationship, you *do* have to learn how to love yourself enough to believe that you are worth being loved. But loving yourself doesn't magically happen overnight.

Chasing the Unavailable, Avoiding the Available

Jade came to me because after years of being in therapy, she still felt hopeless. At forty-six, she had never been in a truly healthy and loving relationship with a man. Jade looks like a *Sports Illustrated* model. She's tall, long-legged, and curvaceous, with thick, wavy auburn hair. I'll never forget our first session. Jade joined our Zoom meeting dressed head to toe in designer clothes, hair blown out, and a full face of thick makeup. She literally looked as though she had just stepped out of a commercial photo shoot. I couldn't resist asking her what the occasion was. After all, she was a single stay-at-home mom, and it was only 10 a.m.

"Wow! Big event to go to after this?" I asked, genuinely curious.

She chuckled.

"No . . . no event. Unless picking up my kids from school is an event?" She laughed nervously. "I just came back from Whole Foods."

"Do you usually wear that much makeup for grocery shopping?"

"Well, sometimes I leave the stilettos behind, but I never leave the house without my hair and makeup done," she said firmly.

My curiosity was piqued. I loved it when I came across important clues about a client's inner world, and I felt I had just found a key puzzle piece but didn't know yet where to place it.

Jade had a long history of chasing emotionally unavailable and wildly inappropriate men. In the past, she would hook up with much younger men who were only interested in casual sex, because she loved the validation of younger men. Most of her romantic relationships were short-lived, except for her marriage, which was essentially a longer version of her other romantic encounters. All of them were filled with what I call "push-pull dynamics": As soon as she got close to a man she was seeing, he would pull away, and she would chase his attention. Then, when he eventually reengaged emotionally and gave her attention, they'd switch roles; Jade would become the one running away from closeness, and her partner would chase her attention. The "push-pull" is the tango of two relationally immature people who aren't aware of their patterns, dancing around intimacy, creating distance instead of closing the gap by building a bridge to each other.

When Jade reached out to me, she had been divorced four years, and her dating history since her split was pretty bleak. She continued to chase aloof, unavailable men because she believed that she had to earn a man's love. In fact, if she didn't have to work hard by looking perfect, acting perfect, or taking care of a man financially, she would think something was wrong with *him* and would end it after three months. She was either chasing the ones who didn't care about her or rejecting the ones who did. Jade offered a perfect example of how, if you don't love yourself enough to see that you are worth being loved, you will sabotage your chances of healthy love.

Because of her years in therapy, Jade understood that having a successful model and actress for a mother—a mother who had to obsess about her own appearance—made it hard for Jade to value herself beyond her looks. Her favorite childhood memories with her mother were going to the makeup counters at Bloomingdale's and learning how to contour her cheekbones with blush and create poutier lips with the right gloss. It meant more to Jade to hear her mother say "That lipstick looks amazing on you" than to hear her congratulate Jade on a paper she wrote for class. What Jade wasn't aware of was that, because her mom struggled to feel worthy due to the unrealistic demands of her profession, she also struggled to keep the long-term love of a good man. Even though Jade's mom beautifully demonstrated how to pursue one's dreams and achieve, she also innocently taught Jade how to overvalue her looks and undervalue who she is and what she has to offer in a relationship. Although Jade had insight into how her upbringing had impacted her self-esteem, she couldn't completely connect the dots between her lack of self-love and her relationships with men. She also didn't know how to break the cycle.

"Jade, I'd like to try a few things to help you raise your self-worth," I said, watching her carefully to see how she reacted to my suggestion.

"Okay . . . like what?" She sounded suspicious.

"After our session, I'd like for you to wash your face and remove all your makeup except for a little mascara and clear lip gloss." (I had to give her *something*.) "Then I want you to put on a T-shirt, jeans, and sneakers and go back to Whole Foods. I don't care if you buy anything or not. You have T-shirts, jeans, and sneakers, right?"

"OMG, yes! I wish I could wear that every day!"

I leveraged her enthusiasm.

"That's great news because for two weeks that's all you're going to wear, unless you're doing yoga." (During our first call, Jade had told me that she loved yoga, but because she was feeling "lazy lately," she hadn't gone in weeks.) "And when you go to yoga four times this week and next, you're not going to wear any makeup, and you're going to pull your hair back in a bun."

Her eyes widened, and she buried her face in her hands, nervously giggling. "Ugh, Jillian, that's going to be hard! What if I see someone I know—what if I see a hot man?"

"I hope you do. Because moving forward, any man you even consider dating has to see *you*."

Forty minutes after our call ended, Jade texted me a selfie of her dressed in a T-shirt, jeans, and sneakers. Her clean, natural, freckled face glowed with just a touch of mascara and clear lip gloss.

"Bravo!" I texted her back.

We Learn to Love Ourselves by Taking Action

In the coaching world, a directive is advice given as an instruction for the client to take action. During our session, I gave Jade three directives: go to Whole Foods wearing just a T-shirt, jeans, sneakers, and minimal makeup; continue to wear that uniform for two weeks; and go to yoga class four times each week, no makeup. A critical step toward self-love is to be true to ourselves instead of exhausting ourselves by pretending to be someone we're not. Jade had spent her entire adult life hiding behind the mask of her thick foundation, fake eyelashes, and shiny lip gloss. Even though she was a jeans-and-T-shirt girl at heart, every morning she dressed as though she was going to a cocktail party. By removing the armor that surrounded her natural self, Jade would slowly train herself to become more comfortable without it.

Jade came to our next Zoom session barefaced, in a worn T-shirt. It was as if I were meeting her for the first time.

"I met someone," she said with a huge grin on her face.

Oy vey, I thought. *Two fucking weeks and she met someone already? I need more time with her! She's not ready!* My mind was a full-blown battlefield of worry.

"Wow, already?" I asked, barely hiding my disappointment.

"Yes! Online. I wasn't even looking, I swear. He reached out, and I thought he was sort of cute, so I agreed to a call. We spoke for three hours. Jillian, what do I do?"

One of the questions I've been asked the most as a relationship coach is "How do I stop attracting unavailable partners?" I always respond, "When you stop choosing them."

The paradox is that when you learn to love yourself, you'll choose emotionally available partners; but it's also true that by making the choice to reject unavailable people and step into the unfamiliar by choosing someone who *is* available to you, you learn to love yourself. The truth is, it's an enormous act of self-love when you no longer pursue the attention of someone who isn't emotionally available to you.

"Well, the first thing to do is to go slow, Jade. He's a stranger who has to audition for the role of dating you, and—"

Jade quickly interrupted me. "What I forgot to mention is that I did a FaceTime call with him and I showed up with no makeup—not even mascara—and my hair was a mess and pulled back! Oh! I was wearing my glasses, too, and an old hooded sweatshirt of mine I usually wear to do laundry!" She laughed gleefully.

I had to admit, I was pretty proud.

"Wait!" She looked stressed. "Does this mean I can't dress up when he takes me to dinner?"

"Of course you can, Jade. This isn't about never wearing makeup and dressing up. I just don't want you to need to do that to feel comfortable in your skin. I want you to feel beautiful all dolled up and also in sweatpants," I reassured her.

"Okay, that makes sense."

"Good. What are you going to wear to your dinner date?"

"I think I'll wear a T-shirt and jeans with a pair of stilettos."

What Does It Actually Mean to Love Ourselves?

As I explained in Truth 1, to be human is to struggle with our value. There isn't a single person who hasn't experienced feeling not good enough. You don't have to love everything about yourself to have self-love. In fact, there are likely things that you dislike about yourself and wish you could change. Welcome to the club. None of us is perfect; we all have bad habits and aspects of our characters that we need to work on improving. But can you accept yourself in spite of your flaws? Can you sit with your ambivalence toward yourself without it turning into hate? Can you commit to trying to be the best version of yourself while also living with the fact that some things may not change? That's the name of the game. It's learning how to stop being so hard on ourselves while simultaneously challenging ourselves to grow and be better people and partners.

Think about someone you love who is not a lover. This person could be a child, a sibling, a parent, or your best friend. What does loving them mean to you? When I reflect on my own understanding of love after helping people for twenty years, it means to appreciate someone for who they are, including all of their nuance and in spite of their messiness (as long as their messiness isn't dysfunctional and causing you and your relationship harm). To love them is to honor everything they have overcome, to see their strengths, to accept their weaknesses, to care about their well-being, and to want the best for them. It also means that we can be angry at them sometimes, but we forgive and we still love them. It also means that when they struggle, we are there for them. It means when they are in pain, we listen.

So, to love yourself means that you appreciate yourself for who you are and all the miles you've walked so far. It means you honor all your strengths and accept your weaknesses. It means you care about your well-being and you want what is best for you. It means that when you mess up and feel ashamed, you forgive yourself. It means that sometimes you'll need boundaries with yourself, but they're ultimately for your highest good. It means when you're in pain, you listen.

How to Actually Love Yourself and Raise Your Self-Worth

The hardest thing about loving ourselves is learning to embrace our flaws while at the same time recognizing that we all have things we need to improve in order to be better people. It's wrestling with the tension that exists between full self-acceptance and the drive to grow and evolve. First and foremost, we *do* have to accept where we are in life, even if where we are is not where we want to be. We can say to ourselves, *Although I wish things were different, I accept that they're not, and I will continue to do my best in trying to get there.*

Ultimately, to love yourself is to see your value in spite of the fact that you're flawed.

But how do we do that?

Climb the Damn Mountain

We have to challenge ourselves in order to raise our self-esteem and see our value.

Every single person needs stability in life. Feeling stable gives us the certainty of knowing that we are safe and have at least some control over our lives. Most people live very safe lives, never challenging themselves to try new things and grow. Most of us can easily get addicted to our routines. And some of us have experienced a lot of instability in our lives, so that we cling to the need to control ourselves, our schedules, and our environments. But the truth is, we need adventure to feel alive, and we need to feel that we're growing so we don't feel stuck in life. In fact, feeling stuck is probably the most common complaint I hear from people who are unhappy, and the only solution is to break up with the familiar and embrace the unfamiliar.

So—whether the mountain is your relationship, a necessary conversation, a flight to a foreign country, pursuing a dream you put on the back burner, finally cleaning out your closet, starting that project that you've been procrastinating on, dating again after divorce, writing the book, apologizing to someone you've hurt, or making a career switch—if you want to raise your self-esteem, climb that mountain.

People think, *When I love myself, I will be ready, and I'll have the confidence, to climb the mountain in my life.* But the truth is, we don't climb the mountain once we love ourselves—we *learn* to love ourselves by courageously climbing it, even when we don't necessarily feel prepared to.

Every time we challenge ourselves to speak up when all we've ever known is staying quiet to keep the peace, every time we walk away from a relationship when our pattern is to stay too long, every time we commit to a relationship when our pattern is to walk too soon, every time we travel when all we've done is remain in our hometown, every time we put ourselves on the line, vulnerable to the unknown, we raise our self-esteem. When we courageously face our fear of the unknown, we say yes to growth. And in that moment, we stretch beyond what we think we're capable of. We feel heroic.

Be Yourself

It's hard to love ourselves if we're not being ourselves.

Social media tells us to be authentic but doesn't tell us how. Jade believed that she had to look and dress a certain way to be good enough. Conditioned by her mother, Jade thought she had to look "perfect" to be accepted by society and loved by men. But her true self was more casual and relaxed. For Jade, being authentic meant wearing very little makeup and comfortable clothes. The more she allowed herself to be herself, the more she could appreciate herself.

Most people are living their lives based on what is expected of them by society, culture, and their families. Consequently, they feel disconnected from themselves.

Becoming a yoga teacher was not what was expected from me. I was born to immigrant parents and was expected to live the American dream: go to college, get a corporate job, and get married. I went to a very respected university my freshman year and was surrounded by girls who ate chocolate cake and then vomited in order to get into a sorority, frat boys who became alcoholics, and professors who hit on me and my friends. When I graduated, I was in a mini crisis; no one told me that it was okay to not know who I wanted to be at twenty-one.

So, I did what was expected of me: I got a job at a huge television news network with amazing benefits and stock options. While there, I was verbally abused by one producer and hit on by another. I had an affair with an anchor. I spent my weekends clubbing and hating Mondays. I got fired because I called in sick too many times and told my mom it was because of company-wide layoffs.

By twenty-seven, I was so lost and disconnected from myself that most days I felt depressed and anxious. I love my parents for wanting me to have a "real" career with a 401(k) and health benefits, because job security is very important and foundational to a less stressful life, but I didn't feel emotionally connected to a conventional career path. In fact, it felt dangerously misaligned with who I was. So, I took a huge risk and quit my job to pursue my dream of becoming a yoga teacher.

Growing up, I had no idea that being a teacher would be an authentic expression of who I am. But when I look back at my life, I can see the clues. I always loved connection and community. At sleepaway camp, I was always picked to be the team captain when we had sports competitions. In my adult years, I've been the person all my friends sought advice from. I've always loved helping people be the best that they can be. Working in the corporate world when I graduated from college was like experiencing a slow death. I later realized that I absolutely hated having a boss—I never was good with authority and always preferred to be the team leader.

Most of us are living our lives based on the "should" model: I *should* be doing this, I *shouldn't* be doing that. We have so many rules about how we and others should live that we easily lose touch with what is truly meant for us. If you're struggling to figure out how to be true to yourself, make a list of all the things that you gravitated toward throughout your life since childhood. Think about the times you have felt most at ease and inspired. What were you naturally good at? What has given you the most fulfillment? What do you feel most emotionally connected to? There are always clues.

To express ourselves more authentically in the world, we need to identify what we feel emotionally connected to. From there, we can explore what makes us feel most at home in ourselves, from hobbies to personal style, interests, friendships, and the kind of work we want to do—whether for money or not.

Stop Talking to Yourself as if You Hate Yourself

Most people have a habit of speaking to themselves harshly. As we learned in Truth 2, our minds can easily become a battlefield of self-limiting stories and judgment that drives us deep into self-contempt. We have to practice speaking to ourselves with more compassion and encouragement in order to love ourselves more. To practice speaking to ourselves with more compassion, we have to become aware of times we're talking to ourselves critically. Changing our self-talk is a practice of mindfulness. It's training ourselves to first notice whenever we're calling ourselves an idiot and then consciously decide to interrupt ourselves midthought. In place of that thought, you say, *No. I'm not going to call myself that.* And then just move on to the next thought. This practice demands diligence and commitment, but as I've said earlier, loving ourselves requires that we take action.

Speaking to ourselves with more care also includes questioning the stories we tell ourselves about ourselves—stories that start with phrases such as "I could never do that," "I always mess up," "I'm not capable of being in a healthy relationship," "Maybe I'm not meant to be loved," "I'm a failed artist," and "I'm too old." The greatest battle we face is the one with ourselves and more specifically, with the stories we tell ourselves about why we don't deserve love or why we can't climb the mountain. These stories keep us stuck, embittered, and lonely. These stories perpetuate low self-worth and need to be challenged, daily.

Author Byron Katie created The Work, an incredibly useful tool to break the pattern of negative self-talk. When stuck in a negative thought, she teaches us to ask these four questions:

1. Is it true?

2. Can you absolutely know it's true?

3. How do you react and what happens when you believe that thought?

4. Who would you be (and I would add, how would you *feel*) without that thought?

The truth is, we must question our limiting, critical, depressing, and blaming thoughts if we want to free ourselves from the mental prison that is self-contempt.

Meet Your Core Needs

The "hierarchy of needs" was first conceptualized by psychologist Abraham Maslow and became a major influence for world-renowned strategic family therapist Cloé Madanes and Tony Robbins. Together, they created human needs psychology.

Human needs psychology is based on the theory that every single person on the planet has six needs that must be met. I've integrated these needs into my personal and professional life, and based on my experience and understanding, I refer to them as our core needs:

The need for safety (this includes the need to feel in control)

The need for adventure (this includes the need for change)

The need for validation (this includes the need to feel important)

The need for love (this includes the need for connection)

The need to grow (this includes the need to be challenged)

The need to give back (this includes the need for purpose)

Even though we all have these needs, how we meet them and what each need means to us will vary from person to person. For example, an adventure for one person could be traveling solo to a foreign country. To another, an adventure is to take the scenic route to work. Feeling secure to one person might mean having a million dollars in the bank, while to another it's having ten thousand in the bank. In my experience as a relationship coach, I've learned that feeling seen and understood in a relationship translates to everyone feeling safe and loved in that relationship. Some people need to be told they're loved every day to feel connected to their partner, whereas others need to be shown that they're loved to feel it. Some people feel most validated when they achieve in their careers, others feel most important when they're giving to their children. If we don't feel like we're growing, we'll feel stuck. Growth happens when we climb the mountain, but everyone has a different mountain to climb. And everyone, whether they know it or not, needs purpose. We find purpose by feeling that we can make a difference in some way. For some that may mean taking care of their children, while for others it's volunteering. When we learn how to meet our own needs more fully and consistently, we teach ourselves how to have our own backs in life and that we don't have to over-rely on others to give us what we are capable of giving to ourselves.

Becoming the Right Partner

We're not going to just wake up one morning and love ourselves. It's a process, and a large part of that process is making decisions that are in our higher interest, support our mental health, and challenge us to grow. Jade, with my help, made the decision to no longer pursue the attention of unavailable men; instead, she made *herself* available to a man with whom she could be herself and to whom she felt a genuine emotional connection. What she didn't expect, however, was that being in a healthy relationship meant that she would have to show up *as* the right partner, not just expect the other to perfectly love her.

It is impossible to fully accept ourselves when we don't maintain a standard for ourselves, which includes how we love and show up for others. Only focusing on our own needs, expectations, and fears in our relationships makes us selfish and reactive, and we sabotage our relationships. On the other hand, when we focus on loving well the people in our lives we care about, we will inevitably feel better about ourselves. It feels good to be a good friend. It feels good to be a good partner.

Two months into her new relationship with Brian, Jade developed some doubts.

"I don't know, Jillian. You don't think it's weird that he likes me so much? I mean I literally wear pimple medicine in front of him. All the other guys I've dated, I've acted so cool around them, and with Brian it's like I don't give a fuck. Maybe I don't like him as much as I *should*?"

I could see the panic in her eyes over FaceTime.

"I find myself getting irritable sometimes when he wants to spend time with me. Then when he's busy, I get insecure that he doesn't like me as much and start to feel needy. I think I'm starting to confuse him because he told me he was starting to feel insecure and stressed-out. *Ugh!*"

She vigorously rubbed her temples in frustration.

Of course he's confused, I thought to myself. If only all the women out there who complained about men being emotionally unavailable and game players knew how often women are guilty of being these things, too.

Unlike Jade, I was expecting her to start doubting the relationship and therefore was well prepared to coach her through this. Jade was just as afraid of intimacy as the men she dated. I knew that once someone truly available walked into her life and wanted to love her, she would resist. Jade was terrified that she wasn't attractive or smart enough for a man to truly love her, and she feared that any man who got close to her would eventually leave. Jade, like so many of us, had a fear of abandonment, and her pattern was to either chase unavailable men or come up with excuses for not committing to the ones who *were* available. Both kept her safe from the risk of heartbreak that comes with opening our hearts to someone and allowing them to truly see us.

This is exactly why self-worth is essential. When we do not see our value, we will scream *Love me! Love me!* to the people who never loved us, and as soon as someone *does* want to love us, we become the emotionally unavailable ones. We'll think, *What's the matter with* them *that they actually want to be with* me?

Jade's fears were dangerously close to screwing up her relationship. She'd become so focused on judging Brian for falling in love with her that she didn't realize she was blocking the very thing she so desperately wanted: love. And not only that—Jade had never been accountable for showing up as a good partner in her former relationships.

I took a deep breath.

"You've finally met a man you're very compatible with and have great sex with, plus he's emotionally and financially stable. You've been brave, and you've shown him the real you, not the fake you who's desperate for validation. There is nothing wrong with him for falling in love with you—in fact, how could he not? But if you keep playing this game where you pull away and judge him when all he wants to do is love you, he eventually will get fed up and he will leave you. And then you'll get to tell yourself the same lies you've been telling yourself for years, which is that men never stay, and they never love you for who you are. I know you're afraid, Jade. I get it, I really do. But you're not being very kind to Brian, and he doesn't deserve that. Look, we have no idea if this guy is your future husband, but so far, this is the healthiest romantic connection you've ever had, so let's work on your anxiety so you can not only receive his love, but you can actually be more loving toward him."

"Holy shit."

That was exactly the response I hoped for.

A year after that conversation with Jade, she and Brian got engaged. This is how I helped her overcome her deeply ingrained fears that otherwise would have sabotaged the relationship:

1. Whenever Jade doubted Brian's feelings for her, her mind became a battlefield of worry and judgment. Once she was aware that this was an old pattern, the most important thing was for Jade to come back to the present so she could calm her anxiety. I instructed her to interrupt her thoughts by taking some deep breaths and going on a drive, listening to her favorite music. (She found driving calming.) I then told her to text me: "The story I am telling myself is . . ." By reading the story she was telling herself, she would instantly be reminded that she was caught in the battlefield, and she could continue to bring her focus back to the present.

2. It's common for people who struggle with their self-esteem to lose themselves when they're in a relationship because they will commonly ignore their own needs and overfocus on their partner's needs. Going to yoga at least four times a week alone or with a friend was essential for Jade to continue doing while in a relationship. She needed to continue to meet her needs without relying on Brian to meet all of them for her. In addition to yoga, I wanted her to see her closest girlfriends at least one night a week without Brian.

3. Jade was relationally inexperienced in her love life. Even though she'd been married, it was a very unhealthy relationship that had little to no communication. I taught Jade how to communicate her needs and fears with more vulnerability, honesty, and compassion, instead of bottling it up and living inside her head. What was even more important for Jade was that she learn how to listen to

Brian. Because of Jade's lack of healthy partnership experience, plus the fact that she struggled with low self-esteem and anxiety, she easily would go into survival mode every time she felt insecure or whenever she and Brian had a disagreement. When this happened, Jade became obsessed with her needs and her need for them to be met. This fixation on herself made Brian feel unseen and made Jade selfish.

Whenever we only focus on ourselves and our needs in a relationship, we become selfish, and selfishness destroys relationships. To love ourselves more completely, we have to show up in our relationships in a way that we're proud of. We have to be "the right partner." That doesn't mean that we don't make mistakes—we will. But when we do, we take responsibility and we course correct.

....

PRACTICING THIS TRUTH

Appreciate everything you've overcome, and challenge yourself, too.

As hard as it might be for you to honor this in yourself, write down every single mountain you have ever climbed in your life, starting from childhood. Remember, the mountain is *anything* that challenged you. Consider all the things, small, medium, and large, you have had to overcome as well as your accomplishments. Situations such as heartbreak, certain achievements, facing fears, a hard childhood, getting into certain programs, completing school or trainings, dealing with challenging or abusive people, career change, work confusion, illness, family illness, financial issues, decisions, directions, and paths.

I've overcome _____.

I survived _____.

I am resilient because _____.

I weathered _____.

I pulled through _____.

I am strong because _____.

I am powerful because _____.

Ask yourself:

1. What are the mountains in your life that you've been hesitating to climb?

2. Do you tell yourself that you're too old or it's too late to do the thing you want to do?

3. How much do you cling to the familiar and avoid the unknown?

4. How would you feel when you reached the top of the mountain— meaning if you took the risk?

5. What did you need emotionally and mentally in order to overcome or achieve the hardest tasks and circumstances of your life?

6. How did they shape who you are today?

7. What are three things you can start doing today to start climbing and create change in your life?

Living Life on Your Terms

Ask yourself:

1. How is what I believe I *should* be doing with my life different from how I actually want to live my life?

2. What do I love to do?

3. What gives my life a sense of meaning and purpose?

4. What gives me a sense of peace?

5. If I weren't trying to please my parents or society, what would I do differently with my life?

Interrupt Your Thoughts

For two weeks, practice catching yourself when you call yourself names. Interrupt the thought. You could say to yourself, *No. I'm not saying that to myself.* Or you can simply replace the thought with something you would say to a child. What you'll notice is that the new thought will be reassuring and encouraging, and over time, being kinder to yourself will become a habit.

How to Better Meet Your Needs

Make a list for yourself of these six core needs:

Safety/control

Adventure/change

Validation/feeling important

Love/connection

Growth/challenge

Giving back/purpose

And then, ask yourself:

1. Which needs do I currently meet for myself?

2. Which needs do I need to focus on meeting more in order to feel more whole and balanced?

3. For each need that you're not completely meeting, what are three new things you can try, to meet those needs more consistently and more fully?

Many people who do this exercise realize that they've been over-focusing on safety and validation and underfocusing on the other needs. All the needs are important, but as I mentioned earlier, living just a safe life will never fulfill us. Here's the hard truth: people who prioritize connection, adventure, growth, and giving back feel better about themselves and their lives. Organize the needs in hierarchical order based on what you know is best for you. For example, experiment with putting giving back as your top need and see how that impacts your life.

Showing Up

Ask yourself:

1. How can I show up for my partner or loved ones better?

2. Can I listen more patiently?

3. Can I meet my loved ones' needs more consistently?

4. Can I be more present for the people I love?

Sometimes I think about what I would say to the younger Jillian who was with David, knowing everything that I know today. I would remind her every single day of just how much she deserves respect and needs to show herself respect, too. I would have hugged her. I would have woken her up from her trance and told her that she needed to be a warrior when it came to her personal boundaries. I would have told her to be brave. I would have told her to focus on herself and her dreams and not to drop everything for a relationship—let alone a relationship with someone who was mean. I would have also told her that what she had with David was not love.

I would have told her never to ignore that voice inside that tells you that something is off with a situation or a person. I would have told her that it was going to take everything that she had to walk away, but that the mountain in front of her was a mountain she was meant to climb all the way to the top. And if I could have, I would have held her hand the whole way up.

When I reflect on that relationship with David now, it's not that I would ever want to go through it again, but I understand its deeper purpose in my life. I know that I would not have the wisdom I have today, and the capacity to help so many other people love themselves, if I had not had that experience.

You Must Speak Up and Tell the Truth

Seven months into my relationship with my ex-husband, we went on a date to *Sleep No More*, an immersive theater experience. I'll never forget how distant he was that night. In the cab on the way to the show, he was quiet.

"Everything okay?" I asked a few times.

"Yes," he replied, growing more annoyed each time I asked. But I knew it wasn't okay. Things were off; he seemed totally disenchanted with me, and I had no idea what I had done to provoke his mood. *Everything was great yesterday*, I thought to myself. *What the fuck happened?* I was confused and felt very uncomfortable. It was a familiar feeling—one I had felt throughout my childhood and adolescence around my father—so I did what was familiar to me: say nothing and quietly suffer with anxiety.

That evening turned out to be one of the strangest of my life.

I used to go clubbing a lot in my teens and early twenties, at dance clubs where the only girls in dresses and heels were drag queens. Men in suits didn't even know these clubs existed. We wore a different uniform: sneakers, loose-fitting clothes, and a I-don't-give-a-fuck-what-anyone-looks-like attitude.

Coincidentally, *Sleep No More* was held at the same venue where I'd spent every weekend of my early twenties. When we arrived, I felt a rush of nostalgia. I was transported to a time when I felt wild and free—the me who loved loud music, strobe lights, and a crowd. I'd dance for five hours straight. I was excited to return with the man I loved and have a fun night.

It was not fun at all.

At *Sleep No More*, they separate you from the person you came with, usher you into a weird elevator, give everyone the same mask to put on (think the movie *Scream*), and when the elevator door opens, you get released into a sea of anonymous drifters. All safe and sound behind our masks, we had permission to follow our voyeuristic instincts as we stood and watched vignettes of peculiar and erotic performance art, loosely based on *Macbeth* and the Hitchcock film *Rebecca*.

Throughout the following two hours, I saw my ex a few times. When I did, I wanted so badly to embrace him, to giggle together, and to compare stories of what we'd seen so far. I wanted to take his hand and complete the night's journey together. But there wasn't even the slightest invitation from him to reunite. Instead, I saw his eyes behind the mask catch mine, and he just kept walking. I was gutted.

I thought he must be testing me to see whether I could be the cool girl and enjoy the night independently, without him. I searched my mind for answers. *Maybe I've been too clingy? Maybe he needs space? But how come yesterday he was all over me and today he's distant?* I continued to ruminate on what I could have done to make him change his mind about me. After the second time he walked past me and didn't acknowledge me, I panicked. I decided to prove to him I was exactly who I believed he wanted: an independent, I-don't-give-a-fuck-if-my-boyfriend-straight-up-ignores-me-on-a-night-out kind of girl. My ego overpowered me, and I wasn't going to let him see my fear and disappointment. I was going to behave exactly the way I thought he wanted me to, so I could prove to him I was still 100 percent worthy of the pedestal he'd put me on.

The mask I wore became more than just an odd novelty. It became the mask that covered up my true feelings. Feelings I was too afraid to trust: feelings of abandonment, anxiety, and worry. I tried to talk myself out of it. *Maybe he's right. I should do this night alone,* I thought to myself. *I love to be alone, dammit.* Was it needy to want things to be good between us before I could actually enjoy myself? Was it needy to want to experience some of the night with him? Fuck. I didn't know. All I knew was that the risk of losing him—this man I wildly loved, whose life felt cemented to mine in just a matter of seven months—was just too much to bear.

So I played cool, acted as if I didn't care, and never called him out on his game.

If I had the confidence to believe my feelings, the presence to honor the discomfort I felt throughout my body (instead of rationalizing my way out of it), and the courage to take off my mask, ending the relationship that night could have been a viable option. And today, I would have. But not before I said this: "Tonight was very hard for me because I felt avoided and tested by you. I need you to know that being avoided is not something I am willing to tolerate moving forward. I know something was bothering you, too. Let's talk about it."

But I did not tell the truth to him that night. I withheld how I really felt, and so did he. We both kept our masks on—even after we were married.

Telling the truth—especially when telling it can cost you your relationship—takes incredible courage.

Telling the truth would become part of my inner work.

I felt hopeless in my marriage. I worked so hard to steady the boat that I lied to keep us together. I didn't betray my husband, but I withheld the truth—my truth—often. I didn't ask for what I needed, I didn't set boundaries, and I didn't share my deepest feelings for fear they would scare him away. Today, I know that we both did the best we could with tools we had—which weren't enough. Like so many couples, we would easily get trapped in a cycle of ineffective communication and un-regulated emotions. Like so many couples, we feared not being good enough, avoided telling each other what we needed, panicked when we didn't get our needs met, and then ultimately blamed each other for our pain.

We know that when our minds become a battlefield, we create stories that make us resentful, and resentment destroys relationships. But so does hopelessness.

Hopelessness comes from feeling disempowered in a relationship because you don't speak up, ask for what you want, and share your feelings. Trust me, I know how hard it is to speak up and have the hard conversations all relationships require. I know what it's like to avoid asking for what you need or expressing your feelings because you're afraid that you'll rock the boat and create too much turbulence. I also know that no relationship is worth building or keeping if we have to lie to keep it.

The truth is, we must be willing to lose our relationship if we want to have any chance at saving it. And sometimes, telling the truth will mean that we *do* lose the relationship, but we might end up saving ourselves instead.

You Have to Speak Up

People avoid the uncomfortable conversations to "keep the peace." But peace isn't the goal of a relationship. Love is. And when we love someone, we have the hard conversations in service of that love.

Like so many people, I avoided the hard conversations because I was equally terrified to hear *his* truth as much as I was to speak my own. This is why relationships take immense courage: We have to risk it all going to hell because if we don't, the alternative is always worse. The alternative is unmet needs, resentment, and self-betrayal. Every relationship, from early dating to long-term partnership, requires speaking up and telling the truth.

We have to ask for what we need, speak up when we don't like something, and ask the questions that may scare us.

To be clear, telling the truth doesn't apply only to serious make-or-break scenarios. We can be honest with ourselves and our partners in small ways every day. Being honest can look like telling a new partner that you're uncomfortable in large social gatherings with a lot of strangers and you prefer smaller get-togethers where you can have more meaningful one-on-one conversations with people. It can look like telling your partner you're really tired and you need a day to rest and reset instead of what you normally have planned on a Saturday afternoon. It can look like telling your longtime spouse that even though you love your tradition of going to dinner once a month, it feels a little stale, and you want to try something new together. We're often held back from being honest on these little things because we worry about the other person's feelings or feel embarrassed, but when we aren't forthcoming, we can end up resenting the other for not giving us what we really want.

There are plenty of people who do not struggle with asserting themselves. But many do. Some learned in childhood that asking for what they want and need would always be met with rejection or hostility. Others were trained by their partners to never speak up because when they did, they were consistently met with confrontation and struggle. Girls and women have been conditioned for centuries to be agreeable, because being sweet and keeping quiet was a way to stay safe and not get in the way. Many struggle with low self-worth and feel unworthy of the things they're asking for. And then there is being too afraid to risk abandonment if we assert ourselves, as I was in my own marriage.

The Elephant(s) in the Room

Michelle and James were a married couple in their early thirties, who came to me because they felt disconnected from each other. When I met them, I was relieved to see that in spite of feeling disconnected, they still appeared to be very bonded. I could tell that they had a strong foundation of friendship: they spoke to each other with respect and without pointing fingers at each other. It was incredibly refreshing to work with a couple who already had mastered the art of accountability and who wanted to do whatever it took to collaborate on a solution to their problem.

Michelle and James had spent the past two years ignoring many elephants, such as his overspending, their borderline abusive relationship with alcohol, and their lack of physical intimacy. They made the decision to invest in couples coaching with me, not realizing how much they were withholding from each other.

I could tell there were things they were not being honest about because they were too afraid to hurt each other's feelings. James had a habit of pleasing; he thought that he had to do everything in his power to avoid disappointing Michelle, which usually meant withholding the truth in some way. Michelle, in her own way, pleased as well, so she didn't have to confront James on what she saw as his lack of direction in life and hurt his feelings.

Additionally, Michelle and James had a communication breakdown, and they used alcohol, as many people do, to brush things under the rug. Cocktails and beers took the place of telling the truth.

Theirs was one of the most important cases I ever worked on, because it was a clear example of how even relationships with a strong foundation can fall apart when we don't tell the truth—and how telling the truth can save a relationship.

When I met them, it was January. They were holding hands, yet I could tell they were feeling uncomfortable. James was looking down, holding his breath. I could also see droplets of sweat form above his top lip and around his brow. Michelle looked a little more relaxed, so I asked her: "How can I help?"

"I feel like I'm with my best friend, but sometimes we're not connecting," she said cautiously.

"How so?"

"Well . . ." Michelle continued to answer my question while looking at James—an indication that she was being mindful of his feelings as she spoke. "I don't really feel like we're present with each other, or that we talk about important things enough, that we're present with each other sexually."

The moment Michelle said "sexually," I saw James freeze. No man wants to hear that his wife isn't sexually satisfied. James looked like someone who had been sucker punched in the gut and was trying to act as if it hadn't happened.

"What do you mean, you're not present for each other sexually?" I asked. As someone who has worked with many couples on their sex lives, one of the most underrated strategies for improving a couple's sex life is to be more mentally present with each other during physical intimacy. I can certainly relate to feeling as though my partner was not really in the room with me; I can also relate to being so distracted myself that I'm not really in the room with my partner. All that does is lead to a lot of disconnection—and lousy sex.

Michelle avoided answering the question. "James is my best friend."

"Yes, I see that," I validated her. "Which is a wonderful thing. You clearly have a very strong foundation beneath you both, as a couple, of friendship and respect. Which is a really good thing. So many couples struggle because they have no foundation."

They smiled warmly at each other.

"I want to feel more connected to James. Sometimes I feel like he's off in another world." Michelle let out a sigh and relaxed back into the couch. She and James were still holding hands, and James still looked like he had been punched in the gut. Interestingly, I don't think Michelle noticed how incredibly uncomfortable James felt.

"Have you ever told him this?" I asked.

She looked at James. "Yes. I mean, a little. We talked about it before we decided to reach out to you." James nodded.

"Look," I said, "I realize how hard this is. You love each other, and you don't want to hurt each other's feelings, which is a beautiful thing. But you're here, and the most important thing is that you are as honest as you can be. Because if we can't talk about the problem, we become the problem. And I get the feeling you two haven't been talking to each other at the level you've needed to."

"It's true," Michelle said quickly. James still looked as if he wasn't breathing. "I think we've gotten into a bad habit of ignoring our problems and using going out and drinking as a way to ignore them." I was struck by the level of self-awareness it took to admit this.

"What do *you* think, James?" I asked him.

I could see how much he was struggling and felt bad for him. "It's okay to be nervous, James. Why don't you stand up, stretch your arms over your head, and take some deep breaths. Then take a sip of water." He did, and when he sat back down, he was much more alert. It never ceases to completely amaze me how effective stretching, breathing, and water are in freeing someone from their emotional discomfort. That said, I knew I had to carefully coach him through emotional expression. He would need my patience and clear direction.

"Um . . . I mean, yes, I have felt that we aren't as connected as we usually are," he said.

James wasn't giving me much to work with, but I could see that he felt very uncomfortable, so I decided to examine this further when I met with him privately.

In private sessions, I learned more about James's history. Raised by an alcoholic father who would often succumb to angry fits and yell at James's mother, James made a decision when he was thirteen years old that he would never be like his father. Instead, he would treat *his* wife like a princess. He would be a nice guy—not a mean, angry man like his father. On the surface, this certainly wasn't a bad decision. But James thought that in order to be a good husband, he had to do whatever it took to never disappoint his wife, even if that meant withholding the truth from her and even if that meant that he was suffering. As Robert Glover writes in his wildly successful book, *No More Mr. Nice Guy*, "Just about everything a Nice Guy does is consciously or unconsciously calculated to gain someone's approval or to avoid disapproval."

James was scared to tell Michelle that he wanted to leave his job and start his own business; he worried that the financial instability would disappoint her. He was scared to hear her say, "That's not a good idea." He was experiencing low-grade depression and anxiety from feeling incredibly stuck in life. When he panicked and got inside his head, he couldn't connect to Michelle. He had no tools to express his inner experience. He also felt paralyzed by his need to please and not disappoint her.

Before James could tell the truth, he had to confront his identity as the nice guy.

He knew he felt stuck, but he didn't know how connected it was to his fear of disappointing her until I pointed it out to him.

When Michelle told me that it seemed as though James was off in another land, she was describing *her* experience of his lack of direction. But really what was going on for James was that he felt trapped between the fear of disappointing his wife and feeling stuck in a job that made him very unhappy.

What I wanted to help them both understand was that their relationship would never reach the depth that it could without open and honest communication. I had to help James see that he would never be like his father and that by withholding his inner world from his wife, he would actually disappoint her *more* than he would if he told the truth. I had to help him build that backbone.

I had to explain the concept of self-abandonment to him.

"No one wants their spouse to abandon themselves to be in a relationship," I told James. "No one who loves you wants you to abandon who you are, in order to be in a relationship with them."

The real work was bringing it into conversation with the two of them.

The next time the three of us were together, I patiently coached James through speaking to his wife in a new way. Some of the direction I gave him was to turn toward her, take some deep breaths, and look her in the eye. I had them hold hands.

To train her to be a safe partner for him, I told Michelle, "This is very new territory for him. I want you to practice true active listening, so you're not plotting your reply or thinking about yourself. You're trying to really hear this person—practicing empathy and compassion right now."

"I'm really, really scared of disappointing you," James said. "I'm afraid that you will think I'm a loser and that I am not the husband that you wanted me to be. And that I will fail you."

I could see Michelle was listening, but she looked confused.

"Michelle, do you have any response to what he just said?" I asked her.

"I love you," she reassured him. "I could never think that you're a loser. I just want to understand what's been going on with you."

"I've been feeling very lost, not really knowing which direction to take, and it's made me really anxious. I feel really stuck."

"This is great," I said, and prodded James to tell Michelle a little bit more about what he was going through. James was flooded with so much emotion that he wasn't used to regulating. I reminded him to take his time and take deep breaths or a sip of water. He continued to tell her about what he was struggling with in his career, knowing that he had a good job but feeling unhappy. He'd always wanted to start his own business, but he'd never discussed it with her, because he didn't know how she'd react.

"I realized when I talked to Jillian that this was making me feel in my head and unmotivated," he told Michelle.

When he finally told his wife about his idea for a business, she was super cool with it.

"Whatever you want to do," Michelle said. "I think we just need to talk about logistics. How much extra work I need to do to support us. I want you to do what's best for you. I certainly don't want you moping around on the couch and not being present with me."

His reaction to her support was like removing the valve of a pressure cooker. All the tension released from his body. Instantly, he relaxed and started breathing again. I felt the relief in my own body when James told her what he wanted.

"Okay, what do you need to be different?" I asked Michelle.

"I need him to take care of his body, and go out and play sports, because that's what makes him happier and more energetic, and that's when I'm more attracted to him."

And what James needed was this: "I need her to put her phone away during dinner and not be working constantly. I would like to actually have quality time with her every evening when we're not both on our phones. I'd like us to do a better job of that."

Then Michelle said, "I want us to stop drinking for a little while because I don't think it's actually good for us. I want us to hold each other accountable, not just brush things under the rug and drink and act like everything is perfect—when things aren't actually perfect and we're not communicating."

He was on board. When they stopped drinking, she started to realize more and more things in the relationship that they had been suppressing and not paying attention to.

There was a cascade of consequences all stemming from the fact that they were not telling the truth to one another. One of those consequences was a dwindling sex life. They didn't talk about their sex life until they came to me. I had to reassure them that this was a conversation that pretty much all couples need to have—whether it's about preferences and dislikes, desires, or needs. As James was able to overcome his fear of disappointing her, they were able to have these conversations more often. For Michelle, she really needed to be able to express disappointment without him freaking out.

Over the course of a year, I helped them tell each other what they'd been avoiding sharing for years. Together, we banished the elephants in the room, and James and Michelle were able to rebuild their marriage with honesty and transparency as their new standard. As painful as it was at times for them to admit to each other, the truth ultimately set them free.

Taking Off the Mask

Cool Girls never get angry; they only smile in a chagrined,
loving manner and let their men do whatever they want.
Go ahead, shit on me, I don't mind, I'm the Cool Girl.
—GILLIAN FLYNN, *GONE GIRL*

Most people place a high value on being authentic, and yet I've worked with and known many people who don't actually honor who they are and are trying to be someone they're not. We may place a high value on authenticity, but if we believe that we're going to be much more seductive being someone else, then usually that's what we'll try to do: be someone else.

Helping people remain authentic when they're afraid they won't find the right person or keep the person they love is what I do most. Because everyone wants love and, as we learned in Truth 1, everyone is afraid that in some way, they're not enough. It takes immense self-awareness and courage to risk rejection and the loss of connection in the name of staying true to who we are and what we value. But the truth is, losing our connection to ourselves has far greater consequences than losing our connection to another. In this section, I will detail what the consequences are for not being completely true to who we are in a relationship.

Go-with-the-Flow Girl

Emma, thirty-seven, didn't want to be single, but she spent years trying to win commitment from a guy who didn't meet any of her needs. When she came to me, she had been to therapy, worked with dating coaches, and taken multiple courses, all in the attempt to figure out how to find love. Nothing seemed to work.

During our first session together, I discovered two patterns that were keeping Emma from the relationship she wanted. First, she remained in casual flings that weren't going anywhere, despite the fact that she wanted a serious relationship, and second, she had a deep aversion to appearing needy—especially in a relationship and when dating.

At work, Emma was confident, assertive, and decisive.

In love, she was go-with-the-flow girl.

Emma's older sibling struggled with addiction, so Emma's role in the family was the "easy child." She went with the flow. Not only did she not demand much attention, but she was extremely accommodating. But that wasn't all. She also had the belief that men prefer "cool girls."

"You know those girls who are always so needy and whiny with their boyfriends? The ones who are *always* complaining? I just cannot be that *girl*," she said with a look of disgust.

She did have a point. There are definitely whiny women *and* men who overwhelm their partners with negativity and demands. But this was different. Emma was under the strong influence of her upbringing and social conditioning, which made her into a pretender. She was pretending to be "cool," which to her meant *I have no needs*. Emma was among countless women who have been hypnotized by this belief and wear the cool, go-with-the-flow mask. I, too, have worn this mask. I wore it at *Sleep No More*, and I continued to wear it when I made the decision to never bring that night up to my ex again.

The go-with-the-flow girl doesn't have needs because that would mean she is needy. Being needy would mean she was unattractive and undesirable. Emma had this belief that to be loved, she had to be easy and cool. She believed she had to be need-less. She didn't know the difference between having needs and being needy. If she didn't like the way a guy was kissing her, she'd act as if she loved it. She faked numerous orgasms because God forbid she tell him how she preferred to be touched. If her feelings were hurt, she could never tell him, because having hurt feelings just meant she was a burden, and being a burden was definitely not cool. Needs aside, she didn't even recognize her basic *right* to ask for a particular restaurant she wanted to dine in, or to request a glass of water when a lover was getting a glass for himself, or even to ask to stop during a road trip so she could pee. She had grown so accustomed to saying "No, I'm good," "Whatever works," and

"Whatever you want works for me" that she lost herself entirely in relationships.

Emma was the "easy child" and I was the "difficult child," and yet both roles had convinced us that having needs made us difficult and unattractive. I was determined to help her break free from the lie just as I had, so she could authentically represent herself and see that telling the truth about who you are is the only way to win the dating game and find love.

"A relationship demands our voice, Emma," I said. "Both people need to bring the gift of their autonomy to the relationship, and part of our autonomy is having needs, opinions, and preferences."

"I hear you, but I just don't want to be difficult, and sometimes it's just easier to not make a big deal out of things."

"Are you like this at work?" She had told me she had a pretty high-powered job in retail marketing.

"Oh God, *no*." Her tone shifted so much that all of a sudden it seemed I was speaking to another woman. "I'm extremely vocal about what I expect from others."

"Okay, so you're saying you don't play it cool at work?"

"That is correct," she declared with not a hint of go-with-the-flow-itis. "But that is work. No guy is going to want to date that part of me."

"Yes, he is," I said, even more confidently. "Is he going to want work Emma all the time? No. But that is part of who you are, Emma. And another part of who you are is actually easygoing! Which is great. In fact, going with the flow and being accommodating and undemanding are good qualities. But not at the expense of your needs. If you're always agreeable, if you're always doing or saying whatever you think the guy would want you to do or say, you're lying to him."

She looked at me, confused.

"Yes, lying," I confirmed. "This is why you keep dating men who aren't the right fit for you, Emma. If you are not yourself in the relationship, which means expressing your wants and needs, then you can't make a real connection with someone. It will always feel one-sided, and you will always feel unfulfilled and, paradoxically, needy for their love."

I could tell she was thinking about what I said.

"Did you feel needy in your last relationship?" I asked her.

"Totally. I couldn't stand it!"

"I get it. You felt needy because your needs were not being met. But that's the thing about being in a relationship, Emma. You have to speak up and tell the truth. Your truth. And that includes your needs and your opinions. Whether it's your need for a commitment, your desire for an orgasm, or your wish to go to a particular restaurant—it all matters."

Emma's biggest challenge when it came to her relationships with men was that she had to learn the difference between having needs and being needy. I explained to her that neediness is expecting our partner to make us happy and secure all the time. Neediness is feeling that nothing our partner ever does is good enough, because we have the unrealistic expectation that our partner should be able to read our minds and never disappoint us. Neediness is forfeiting all our self-sufficiency and making it someone else's responsibility to take care of our needs at any given moment, as if we were a child. As psychologist and philosopher Erich Fromm wrote in *The Art of Loving*, "Immature love says: 'I love you because I need you.' Mature love says: 'I need you because I love you.'" Neediness isn't about loving the other person. It's about needing just about anyone who will make us feel better because we don't know how to make ourselves feel better.

The Cool Girl, the Good Girl, and the Nice Guy

A "cool girl" goes with the flow because she wants to be seen as "chill." Nothing bothers her. Sick of the ole ball and chain? Cool girl to the rescue. Sick of having to show up and give emotional support to your girlfriend? Cool girl to the rescue. Sick of meeting women who want a real relationship? Cool girl to the rescue.

If I could narrow down two destructive archetypes that plague many women of all ages, it would be the "cool girl" and the "good girl." On the outside they appear different. The cool girl is more likely a chameleon—she'll shape-shift herself into being whoever she believes "they" really want. She's the girl who can hang out with the boys and watch football and then transform into a porn star later on in the bedroom. She's the girl who will pretend she loves the outdoors and camping even though she hates the outdoors and would much rather stay in a five-star hotel. She's also the girl who will act as though nothing fazes her—even if you never make her a priority in your life.

The good girl is typically sweet, agreeable, and a nurturer. She follows all the rules and is polite. Her belief system says, *If I have boundaries, then I'm unkind. If I have a strong opinion, then I'm aggressive. If I have needs, then I'm selfish.* As much as I think most people could learn how to be more selfless in their relationships and not always make everything about them, the good girl is selfless to a fault. Not only does she put everyone else's needs and comfort before her own, but the good girl is also at risk of making excuses for horrible behavior.

What the cool girl and good girl have in common is that they both have almost nonexistent boundaries, and like Emma, they pretend they don't have needs in order to be "good enough." They both unconsciously believe that if they speak up and tell the truth about how they feel, what they need, and what they want, they will be rejected and unloved. So they lie. They lie because they are influenced by the conditioning that a woman with needs, opinions, and fears is a difficult woman. They lie because they believe that to tell the truth means they could be seen as bitchy, whiny, needy, masculine, cold, or annoying. In other words, you're either cool or you're difficult. You're either sweet or you're a bitch. You either have no needs (or very few) or you're needy. The cool girl and the good girl live in a world of harsh binaries, not understanding that we are all much more complex than movie characters.

In the film *The Devil Wears Prada*, Miranda Priestly (played by Meryl Streep) shows us that to be a powerful woman is to be a bitch. We sympathize with weak, vulnerable Andy (Anne Hathaway), the archetypal good girl, but we also know that she desperately needs a transformation. At the beginning, Andy wants to please and will do anything to fit herself into the roles she's been assigned. As the audience, we want to see the underdog win, but we also want to see the people pleaser, who is at the beck and call of the villain, find herself and step into her power. The whole movie is about Andy finding her backbone and her voice—and, in doing so, she ultimately overcomes good girl syndrome and finds herself. Her hero's journey ends with her coming out on the other side, finally leaving the job, and pursuing her own passion.

James, whom you met earlier, was the typical "nice guy." The nice guy, just like the good girl *and* the cool girl, lies in order to avoid rejection and gain validation and love. Healing the impulse to please varies from person to person, but as we saw with James, *his* healing meant unlearning the belief that a man is either aggressive and unhinged or nice and basically without opinions. He needed to learn that he could be kind and loving while still having his own needs and feelings. He needed to learn that he could be accommodating without compromising his values, needs, or dreams. Healing meant learning how to lean into his discomfort, pursue his dreams, and communicate.

Emma's unconscious strategy to seduce men was to go with the flow. She thought this would get men to be interested in her, even though it wasn't long before she realized that none of them ever seemed to be entirely invested in her emotionally. Her story was *no man ever truly loves me*—a story that, not surprisingly, lowered her self-worth and made her question her lovability. She didn't realize that her seduction strategy was deeply flawed. She didn't know that the greatest seduction happens when we lean into our realness, because the confidence to be ourselves is what ultimately attracts the right people into our lives.

Emma's work was to bring the more confident, self-assured parts of herself to dating and a potential relationship. I had her do this with consistent practice, beginning with asking for what she needed in small, basic ways (such as making restaurant or activity requests with dates). Each week, we would talk about the discomfort she would face in asserting her presence and voice even in these small ways. But thankfully, Emma didn't allow her discomfort to stop her. She continued with these baby steps until making requests became easy for her! Once she got used to being vocal about her preferences within the dating process, it was then time to help Emma make better choices in her love life.

Previously, Emma had settled for casual relationships with men she wasn't that interested in. According to the go-with-the-flow part of her, it was too difficult to set boundaries and much easier to let these "relationships" fade out and run their course. The problem was that she was wasting time. She wanted to get married and start a family. Spending time with men she wasn't that interested in was keeping her from meeting the right person for her.

"It's time to clean house, Emma," I said directly. "Sticking around is only wasting your time and theirs. You can actually have what you want. You just have to demand more for your love life, the way you do for your work life."

"Okay, but I have no idea what to say to them!"

And this is when it really struck me. So many of us lower our standards, struggle to enforce boundaries, and hide from the truth simply because we don't know how to communicate.

"What would you say if you weren't afraid, Emma?" I asked gently.

She paused. "I think I would just be direct and tell them that I've enjoyed our time together, but this is not a match for me."

"I think that's perfect, Emma." I smiled. Seemingly small breakthroughs like this moment give my own life so much meaning.

Telling the truth will often take an enormous amount of courage. The truth is often hidden underneath layers of our subconscious patterns (think cool girl, good girl, nice guy) created to protect ourselves from being hurt. When we believe that by telling the truth we might be seen as weak, a failure, or unattractive, it becomes really easy to conceal the truth. Additionally, when we lack the tools to express ourselves, we can get trapped in the battlefield of our minds and become resentful. Don't overthink it and overcomplicate it. It's just the truth. It will free you. The truth has the power to steer a struggling relationship back on track. The truth will help us leave something that isn't right or start a new relationship on honest, healthy ground. So instead of focusing on another's transparency, raise the standard for yourself. Don't play small anymore—play really big by telling the truth to yourself first, then bringing your authenticity to everyone you relate to. You no longer need the mask. The truth is that the most valuable thing you can bring to a relationship is the truth.

. . . .

PRACTICING THIS TRUTH

If you seek love, be yourself.
—BECCA LEE

As you learned in this chapter, the consequences of not telling the truth have massive repercussions not only for our relationships with others but also for our relationship with ourselves. These consequences are resentment, disconnection, and the utter disempowerment that comes from losing ourselves to fear instead of expressing who we are and what we feel.

How to Assert Yourself in a Relationship or When Dating

There is no need to puff your chest and challenge someone to a debate. Your only job is to stand your ground for truth, not your ego, because the truth is what elevates relationships. You can do this with vulnerability *and* resoluteness, and you will need to work with your breathing so you can self-regulate. To prepare, it's important to take deep, long, slow breaths and focus on a slightly longer exhale to release any tension and anxiety you may have. If you pay attention, you might notice that most of your tension lives in one location, such as your stomach, chest, jaw, or hands. Keep actively trying to let go of that tension with each subsequent breath out.

Examples of self-assertion:
_____

"I've enjoyed getting to know you, but I don't feel a romantic connection. I wish you the best of luck."

"I prefer not to text when getting to know someone and instead have an actual phone call."

"I love you, and I want us to work. And I need some things to change in order for me to be able to thrive in this relationship." (Then clearly state one to three things you need to be different.)

"I didn't like how that made me feel. I feel hurt. Can we talk about it?"

"Please tell me what you need from me in order to have a productive conversation. This is what I need: _____."

"I really like you, and I'm so attracted to you. But I'm not interested in casual sex. I'm looking for a meaningful connection with someone I can build a life with, so I prefer to wait until we know each other a lot better before we bring sex into the equation."

"I really like you and would like to see more of you. What do you think?"

"What I would prefer is _____."

"This simply doesn't work for me. What I need is _____."

"I could really use a hug. I want to feel more connected to you."

How to Tell the Truth When It's Hard

When in a relationship, the goal of a hard conversation must be connection and love. To reach this goal, we must prioritize making the other feel seen and heard. We also must be honest. If the goal is to "win" the conversation, it will yield more disconnection.

In an uncomfortable conversation, we feel uncertain of what the outcome will be. Having one of these conversations usually means we are going to have to say and hear things that might feel like a lot to process. We might fear being misunderstood and unheard. We might fear rejection. Again, it is important to remember the higher purpose for the conversation—whether it is to rebuild connection, express your feelings, or share what your boundaries are—and to try to remain as present as possible by breathing, focusing on a longer exhale when you feel tense.

It is also important to focus on telling the truth, leading with both vulnerability and directness.

Examples for dating or early relationships:

"I've been in my head lately, and I really want to be more present. Some things have been bothering me that I haven't been so honest about. I am so sorry. Can we talk about them now?"

"I care so much about you, but I feel like we've done the best that we can, and I think that it's better for us to go our separate ways. I know that this is very difficult, but I'm feeling that this is best for me and ultimately for both of us."

Examples for couples:

"I'm struggling in our relationship. I don't feel understood or seen. And I'm sure you don't feel that way, either. Can we talk about this?"

"I know you want to talk, and I promise I am not going anywhere. I just need a few minutes to gather my thoughts, because I feel overwhelmed. Okay?"

"My last relationship was hard because _____, so sometimes I get insecure during _____, but I'm doing my best to stay present. I wanted you to know because it really impacted me."

If you feel an argument brewing, you can say, "I feel like this is starting to escalate, and I care about us too much to allow this to get out of hand. Let's take a little time-out to calm down, and we can resume in a few minutes, okay?"

How to Be Yourself if You're Dating

Answer these questions:

1. How do you strategize to get someone to be interested in you?

2. What if you made authenticity your goal? What would change?

Most people have one goal when they're attracted to someone: get this person to be attracted back, and do whatever is necessary to make that happen. The primitive part of us has one objective: *Get love.* It's not rational—it's survival. This is the reason Emma and countless others will be chameleons when they meet someone they like. They'll contort themselves into being whoever they think will please the other person in a strategic attempt to receive validation, acceptance, and attention.

But, as you learned with Emma, this is a major reason you might not be attracting and choosing the right people. The truth is, authenticity is what attracts the right match for you and repels the ones who are not the right match. Authenticity is the most reliable sifter and sorter of potential mates.

If you want love, you have to represent yourself, not sell yourself out.

When you feel anxious, practice breathing and relaxing your body, and then stay present and see whether you have some things in common with this person. Notice when you attempt to appear "cool" and, instead, be a little vulnerable. Share about something meaningful for you, whether it's your family, art, travel, a cause, or your pet. Anyone who is unresponsive to your realness is not a match.

What makes a relationship work is authenticity and telling the truth. Lies make a relationship dysfunctional. But we don't talk enough about the amount of courage it takes to be authentic, to express our needs when we think our needs might be rejected, and to assert ourselves when we think asserting ourselves might mean the end of the relationship. It takes an enormous amount of courage to tell the truth, because we must be who we are, instead of who we think we're supposed to be. And we must speak up, even when it scares us.

_____

You Need to Be Your Best Self
(Even After the Honeymoon)

I can do nothing for you but work on myself . . .
you can do nothing for me but work on yourself.

—RAM DASS

Lauren's email read, "I need help in becoming a better person so I can get my girlfriend back."

She asked whether we could have an emergency session. Her girlfriend, Jess, had just broken up with her, and in two days they were planning to meet and discuss their relationship.

"When I first met my girlfriend, it was like I became the best version of myself," Lauren told me when I met her over Zoom. "Instead of stressing out all the time over the littlest things, I would be much calmer and positive about things. I would work out every day because I really wanted to be my best self for her *and* me."

At thirty-one, Lauren had a larger-than-life vibe—the kind that felt very energizing to be around. She used her hands like a maestro conductor when she spoke and had a distinctive, infectious laugh.

She continued: "Then, I don't know. I just let all my usual bullshit get in the way. My stress, family crap. I got moody. I'd complain about work to her constantly and spend the weekends binge-watching TV instead of wanting to go out and do things with her. When Jess would try to snap me out of it, I would bitch that she didn't understand me and that I didn't feel seen. Instead, it was *Jess* who didn't feel seen. I just became lazy about taking care of myself."

There's an old saying: "Everyone is on their best behavior in the beginning of a relationship." This explains why the first few weeks or months of getting to know someone are often referred to as the "honeymoon period." We bring our A game in the beginning. We bring flowers. We cook dinner. We plan dates. We dress up for dates. We work out and take care of our bodies. We want to be the most seductive, caring, mature, interesting, multidimensional person that we can be. We are our best selves: we're fun, we listen, we are adventurous, we're in a good mood. We say "Yes!" to new experiences. And we are curious and inquisitive. We ask our partner questions and make them feel like the only other person in the room.

But once we get comfortable, we stop trying, and that's when problems begin to surface in a relationship. The truth is, we stop trying to be happy, present, interested, and fun. Instead, we fall back into the familiar emotional patterns we've had for years and perhaps even decades before meeting this person. We get stressed and bring our stress home to our partner, while we're on our best behavior with friends and co-workers. We become pessimistic and apathetic, when we used to be full of life and positive.

Loving, fulfilling relationships are determined by two things: whom we choose to love and how we choose to show up. We must always strive to become the person we'd want to be in a relationship with. Because we can write down all the important traits we want in a partner, raise our standards, and not settle, but if we don't search inside ourselves and strive to become the person we'd want to be in a relationship with, we won't be any closer to the relationship we hoped we'd have. The person willing to look in the mirror and grow is closer to the relationship that they want.

Inside all of us is a child who desperately yearns to be loved by a partner the way a parent would ideally love us: unconditionally. Romantic love always comes with conditions. We can't be consistently moody, stressed-out, and uncommunicative, and expect someone to just love us anyway.

When Lauren was finished talking, I asked her, "Have you done this before in your previous relationships?" I was pretty sure what her answer would be.

"Yeah." She sunk back into her chair, which made her look smaller and defeated.

"You got comfortable-itis," I said with a grin.

"Huh?"

"You got comfortable and started treating Jess as though she would never leave you."

"That's exactly it!" Lauren sat straight up. "How do I cure it? Maybe I need to go on a yoga retreat."

I burst out laughing. As a former yoga teacher who had led several retreats, I was well aware of how many people went on retreats to "heal." To be fair, a good yoga retreat can help us with a profound physical, mental, and spiritual reset, but it's not the answer to breaking relational patterns. Lauren was able to manage her emotional states much more effectively in the beginning because she was motivated by her new relationship. But, as many of us do, she lost the motivation because she thought that the relationship would stand strong on its own. We become complacent and fall back into familiar patterns. But what if we could stay motivated for ourselves *and* for the relationship, months and years into it?

Lauren never had a problem attracting lovers. Her larger-than-life energy was like an aphrodisiac to many women, and her warm and playful attentiveness toward them added to her seductive charm. But all four of her relationships—including the one with Jess—ended after a few months. Each one shared a similar story: they started out strong; a few months in, Lauren would stop being her warm, playful, and energetic self; her partners would get frustrated; they would start to fight; and they would eventually break up. This time, Lauren had already figured out that the common denominator in her relationships was her. It wasn't that her girlfriends were perfect by any means, but Lauren had the self-awareness to understand that she had a destructive relational pattern.

You might be thinking that Lauren was a type of narcissistic love-bomber—someone who premeditates their seductions by strategically giving potential lovers attention and praise, only to discard them once they "get" them. Or that Lauren was inauthentic and overperformed to get people to like her, and then once she was comfortable, the "real" Lauren came out. The truth about Lauren, however, was that her real self *was* warm, funny, playful, and energetic. She was also, just like all of us, susceptible to stress and to handling it poorly. But most important, Lauren had been unaware that her emotional states impacted her relationships and that no one was responsible for them but her.

The truth is, we are responsible for how we show up in our relationships. We must never stop pursuing the things that light us up and give our lives meaning just because we're in a relationship. And here's the harder part for most of us: we have to bring that light home to our partner instead of spreading it just to friends, coworkers, or strangers. When we consistently give the best part of ourselves to everyone but our partners, we slowly destroy the relationship.

"You don't need a yoga retreat, Lauren, and you don't need to become a better person. You just have a bad habit of taking your relationship for granted and thinking that you can get away with it. You, like so many of us, forget that a relationship needs to be nurtured, and we nurture it best by nurturing the relationship we have with ourselves. Your partner isn't responsible for taking your stress away," I said.

"Oh my God!" Lauren yelled. "This is exactly my parents. They are so grumpy with each other. I mean they managed to stay married for forty years, but I never saw them really love each other, you know? For as long as I can remember, they bickered. They're not that, like . . . *warm* with each other. Also, to be honest, both of them are *total* stress cases. Mom is always stressed about nothing. Dad is always stressed about work. It's always been that way."

"Sounds like your parents, like so many of our parents, didn't have the tools to manage their stress and overwhelm—that's a big insight about your childhood, Lauren." I praised her. "So now, you have an opportunity to do things differently. You're aware now. I will give you some tools. All you have to do is use them. You just need to be diligent about doing the things that help you feel more balanced and then consistently bring that good energy to your relationship. But remember, Lauren, you will sometimes be in a bad mood. You will be stressed sometimes and feel down. You're human. The key is to be much more mindful about not burdening your relationship by not taking care of yourself and expecting your partner to just deal with it. You don't expect your coworkers to *just deal with it*, right?"

"No, never," she admitted.

Two days later, Lauren met up with Jess and apologized for taking her for granted and for expecting her to make her feel better.

Three weeks after our call, Lauren let me know that she and Jess had happily gotten back together. But Lauren had not simply repaired her relationship; she had also done the hard work of repairing other pieces of her life to excavate the higher version of herself from within. I received this letter from her:

Dear Jillian,

I wanted to sincerely thank you for helping me save my relationship with Jess. But if I'm being honest, what you really did was help me with my relationship with myself. Since our conversation, I took a long, hard look at myself in the mirror and realized that I had been sabotaging all my relationships my whole adult life. I would expect my friends to love me even though I would go days without returning their texts and break plans with them all the time. Every time I went home for the holidays, I would turn into a grumpy ten-year-old and be unpleasant to be around. At work, I was present, attentive, and kind, and as soon as I got home to Jess, I would act like she was a nuisance and I just wanted to be alone. So I followed your advice, and I made some changes. I started addressing

my stress. I now meditate every single day, started eating better
(fewer sugar and caffeine crashes now!), and started swimming four
days a week. I feel so much better. I also started treating the people
I love like I could lose them at any time—just like you said to. It has
helped immensely. Jess and I are going strong.

Thank you, Jillian, for showing me the mirror. I will always be
grateful.

Lauren

That was three years ago, and Lauren and Jess are still together.

The Mirror

Romantic relationships are a mirror: they show us where our work lies. And everyone has their work to do. We're all tasked with working hard to overcome behaving like a child every time we're triggered. We have to work hard to heal parts of our pasts. We all have to work to be accountable when all we want is to blame others. I don't know a single person who doesn't need to learn better communication skills and work to implement them. People think that if they finally meet that "right person" or their partner finally changes, then they won't have work to do. It's not true. Even with the best partner in the world, we will still have to face ourselves—and in doing so, we have to confront generations of conditioning, passed down from our own families and society. Conditioning that's convinced us that it's unsafe to be vulnerable and open our hearts because we might be abandoned or someone might want to change us. Conditioning that's taught us that we don't have to treat our partner like a gift but instead treat them like a given. Conditioning that's trained us to believe that "The One" is responsible for making us happy.

Choosing a person to spend your life with is one of the most important decisions you ever make. In fact, consider all the important decisions you have ever made and add them all up—most of them will never match the importance of deciding with whom to spend your life. But equally important is the decision to show up as your best self more consistently. A very common reason people repeat patterns in their relationships is that changing partners is often not enough of a solution. We take ourselves wherever we go. So while a new partner might be *very* necessary, we have to choose that partner as a person who has looked in the mirror and faced the challenge of growing.

Your Lower Self vs. Your Higher Self

None of us is perfect. All of us have pain and bad habits. And everyone has the fear that they are not enough in some way.

Inside everyone is a scared child desperate for love and to feel safe. But you also have inside of you a wise awareness that is certain—and certain of its value. Call it your inner voice, your intuition, the wise parent, the healer, the sage, or the mystic. Or call it your higher self. This is the part of us that isn't constantly searching for control and to feel good enough. Instead, it is often calm, present, and confident. Sometimes, it's playful and passionate. It is the part of ourselves that responds instead of reacting. It is the part that chooses love over fear and would prefer to move on instead of holding on to grudges. It is the part of us that is kind and compassionate toward ourselves and others.

Your higher self knows it is enough. It takes risks and is willing to be vulnerable. Your best self communicates honestly. It focuses on repairing connection after conflict instead of blaming. It listens to others and sincerely apologizes when it has made a mistake. Your higher self seeks to understand others instead of judging them. It has a sense of humor and doesn't take itself too seriously. Your higher self knows what is best for you; it knows what makes you happy and what is standing in the way of your peace.

Your higher self is your most authentic self, and it is *always* available to you. And mine is always available to me.

As I said in Truth 2, the greatest battles we face are with ourselves. Being our higher selves is not always easy. It takes discipline, and most important, it takes a strong, unwavering desire to feel and be better. The more we can search inside ourselves, find that wiser, kinder, and more stable part of ourselves, and give it the steering wheel, the better our relationship with ourselves will be. And the better our relationship is with ourselves, the better our relationship with another will be.

It's a lot easier to be our best selves when we're with certain friends, helping a stranger, or alone doing what we love to do. But it becomes a whole other challenge when we're triggered by a lover, a partner, or especially a family member. How we respond to a trigger is the ultimate test of our maturity, and we *will* fail that test many times. Learning to respond from our higher self rather than reacting from our fearful, vengeful, or self-righteous lower self takes a lot of self-awareness and even more practice. I will give you tools on how to practice this skill at the end of this chapter.

We all have pain. Everyone has trauma, and some of us have been stuck in survival mode for so long that we have forgotten what it's like to not constantly be searching for security. (I will address this problem at the end of the chapter.) Additionally, much of social media has trained people to be obsessed with needing validation to feel good about themselves. Constantly comparing one's own life, body, and relationship to another's has made people become totally consumed with themselves and how they look instead of focusing on becoming better people and helping others. Our insecurities, pain, and fears are all part of being human, but they also mean we each have a lower self that can be immature, spiteful, jealous, and insecure. When we're pushed to the edge of our insecurity, and when all we focus on is needing to feel validated and significant, we can easily behave in ways that are below our character.

Our lower self is the part of us that sabotages. Our inner saboteur will punish our partner for the mistakes that our terrible ex made. We'll blame our partner for making us feel insecure, when feeling insecure is how we entered the relationship. We'll shut down because that is what Dad did. We'll criticize because that's what Mom did. We'll people please because that's what we did as children, and it worked back then. When it comes to being a mature adult in a relationship, it's crucial that we become more aware of when we're seeing, judging, reacting, and experiencing our partner or lover through the filter of our pasts.

Our higher self always takes responsibility for our projections and unfair blaming and punishing. When we are in our higher self, we are able to say, "It is not you. It is me. It's my fear, my trigger. I'm sorry. I love you." This is the work we all have to do—always.

Every couple I've ever worked with has come to me because one person believes the other person needs to change, when the secret that most relationship coaches and therapists know is that, more often than not, if you want to change the other, it begins with you.

Jason and Rachel, a couple in their midthirties who found me on Instagram, came to me for help, each believing the other was the problem. Although I knew they were both good people who wanted to do better, working with them felt like working with two sixteen-year-olds trying to save their relationship.

According to Jason, every time he and Rachel would get into an argument, she would blame him and push him away. She would need space and question the relationship, which would trigger his insecurity. Jason thought that Rachel acted as if every argument was his fault, and he didn't think she took responsibility for her contributions to their problems.

According to Rachel, Jason was uptight. She liked to go with the flow, and he liked control. He would be rigid about plans and inflexible when they had arguments. One of Rachel's biggest complaints was that he never really listened to her. When she spoke, he was somewhere else.

As much as we like to think otherwise, we attract people who are at the same level of maturity and consciousness as we are. Even though Rachel and Jason were two very different people, with different approaches to conflict, they still were very, very immature. They believed that the other person was the problem and didn't want to take responsibility for their role in the dynamic that wasn't working between them.

On Zoom, I noticed a lot of snide remarks and eye rolls from both of them. There was a lot of interrupting. Neither was listening to the other. These were two people in a lower-self relationship. They felt totally unseen and unheard and were treating love as though it were a trade: *I'll scratch your back, but only if you scratch my back first. If you're going to be a bitch, I'm going to be a dick.* Their inner saboteurs had the steering wheel. They were punishing each other, not taking responsibility, and focusing only on their own needs without paying attention to the needs of the other.

I said, "Tell me about a time when the two of you were getting along really well."

Jason described the previous weekend. "I picked her up, and we went to her favorite place for lunch. We were laughing, just goofing around, took a great drive up the coast. We were relaxed. She was in a good mood. I was in a good mood. We just were enjoying life together."

When I looked at Rachel, she was nodding along in agreement.

"So tell me about when it goes south for the two of you," I said.

"Well, just the other day, I woke up not feeling that great. I had my period. I had a really, really hard day at work," Rachel said. "I wasn't in the mood to do anything. I just wanted to go home and chill. When we spoke that evening over the phone, he kept on asking me, 'What's wrong? What's your problem?' Like he was annoyed at *me* for not being in a good mood. I just wanted him to leave me alone."

"I did leave you alone."

"Yeah, but then you didn't call me for, like, *two days*. And you usually call me multiple times a day."

Jason rolled his eyes.

I watched their lower selves nitpick and play tit for tat right in front of me.

"Stop. If you could only see yourselves. Aren't you exhausted?" I asked them.

They both looked at me like deer in headlights.

"It's time to do something different," I said. "You're going to stand up. Jason, go take a walk around the block. Rachel, go drink a glass of water and take a few minutes alone in your bedroom to breathe and calm down. When you come back in five to ten minutes, I want you to come back as seventy-five-year-olds who have lived a full life and realize that they don't have many years left."

They did.

When they sat back down, I reminded them, "You're in your mid-seventies, you have grandkids. At this stage of life, you know what really matters and what doesn't. You've had friends die, parents die. You've had many life experiences, and you are more aware than you've ever been of your own mortality. What do you want to say to each other?"

Rachel began, "I feel like you always—"

I stopped her and reminded them about my rules for communication: Use "I" instead of "you." Avoid using the words "never" and "always," as well as the phrase "you made me feel."

"I want you to focus on what *you feel*, not what *he's doing*," I said.

Rachel started again. "I sometimes feel overwhelmed and sad because I don't think you understand me. Sometimes I just want to be able to have a hard day and not have to worry about how my hard day is going to stress you out."

He started to interrupt, and I said, "You're not allowed to interrupt right now. You become a safe partner when she can share her feelings with you, without fearing that you're going to judge her or dismiss what she's feeling."

"Sometimes I get overwhelmed because I'm someone who likes to go with the flow, and when you're going with the flow with me, I think we have a really good time together, but I get frustrated when you get rigid and I don't know how to handle it. And that's something that I need to work on."

I praised her for taking responsibility for what she was struggling with.

"And so when I'm overwhelmed, the easiest thing for me to do is to push you away, because then I don't have to deal." Rachel started to tear up. She told me, "I feel very rejected, and then my impulse is just to get angry and push him away."

While she was talking, I was watching Jason very carefully. I was watching his body language for any kind of reaction. I was watching him breathe. When I saw his body tense up and get reactive, that's when I reminded him to relax his body, really listen to her, and attune to her pain, rather than plot his reply. I was having them practice empathy: speak to each other differently and respond with compassion.

When we are accountable and communicate our feelings instead of blame, we make it easier for our partner to empathize with us. We block empathy when all we do is blame each other.

Then I had Jason repeat back what he heard. He admitted, "I think that she's right that I often am a bit of a control freak and I can get in my head. If she's not in a good space, then it's like the room is really messy and I can't fix it. There's a part of me that shuts down to her."

Finally, there was some self-awareness coming to the surface.

Jason told Rachel, "I realize now that when I feel you push me away, I just want to punish you, by not being as attentive toward you or just acting like I don't care. And I get very frustrated when you have a lot of mood changes. I guess I don't really understand it. And then I think that I did something wrong to *make* you be in a bad mood, and *then* I'm afraid that you're just going to push me away so much that we break up. If I'm honest, I just want to get back at you and make *you* feel as insecure as *I* feel."

I was very impressed with his honesty. Perhaps not all was lost between these two.

The truth is, people are not motivated to change their behavior when they feel punished; they're motivated by positive reinforcement. You're never going to get your partner to change with punishment, and you're never going to be able to get more love by "getting back" at them.

Ultimately, I helped Rachel and Jason learn how to communicate more honestly with each other, stop the blame game, and grow up.

I assigned Jason to make space for Rachel to have a full range of emotions. And when she was in a bad mood, for whatever reason, to not take it so personally and not try to fix it.

Her assignment was to be more communicative when she was in a bad mood, instead of just pushing him away. I encouraged her to ask for what she needed, instead of shutting down.

Their assignment as a couple was to be kinder in their communication with each other, to reassure each other, and to stop punishing each other. I knew this wasn't going to be easy and that growing up doesn't happen overnight. They both had to *want* to be their higher selves in the relationship. If they didn't have that standard for themselves, they would not have changed.

I gave them the assignment to use a specific code word of their choosing when one or both of them noticed that they were falling back into their old pattern. Then they would have to take a break and come back as their wiser, higher selves.

A great pattern interrupter is humor. Since they both had a similar sense of humor, I encouraged them to use humor sometimes to break the pattern. Laughing is what brings people into the present moment.

If I'm honest, as impressed as I was with their self-awareness, I wasn't really sure whether they had the maturity yet to break this pattern. But I knew that if they did the work now, it would serve them in future relationships.

We cannot improve our love lives if we do not acknowledge and confront the saboteur that lives inside of us. Everyone has an inner saboteur, and it's usually the teenager (or younger child) part of ourselves, who is always looking for ways to self-protect from hurt. Because the immature and wounded part of ourselves is always desperately searching for safety, it will destroy anything that stands in the way of finding it.

Our inner saboteur has the purest of intentions: to protect us from hurt. Therefore, if we just reject or hate that part of ourselves, we make it impossible to fully accept and love ourselves. Once we understand its intent, then the wiser part of ourselves can intervene and become a mentor, or a parent, to the inner saboteur and acknowledge its feelings and pains, without letting it take the steering wheel.

Some saboteurs will ghost or avoid communication. Some will cheat. Some, like Lauren's inner saboteur, will get too comfortable and stop trying. Others, like those of many of my clients, will chase unavailable men and question the character of the available ones. Then there are the saboteurs like Jennifer's, in Truth 1, whose jealousy caused many unnecessary arguments with her partners.

The only way to protect our relationships from this part of ourselves is to be aware of its existence, thank it for trying to keep us safe, and then, after a deep breath, gently yet intentionally step out of it and up into our higher selves.

Fear, Selfishness, and the Punisher

To love a selfish person is to suffer. When we refer to someone as "toxic" or as having narcissistic tendencies, what we're really describing is someone who only thinks of themselves and what they can get from others. But a really hard truth is that even the most loving and generous person in the room can be selfish at times, especially when they're afraid that they will lose the love and attention of the person they care about most: specifically, their romantic partner. This is the reason we have to acknowledge how we can sometimes be selfish in a relationship. This is what it means to be self-aware.

Our relationships determine our happiness in life. Even if we have our physical health, our work is going well, and we have money in the bank, if our most important relationships are struggling, we will suffer. Very specifically, when our romantic relationship is strained—if we feel insecure, hurt, or fearful that the relationship could end—we'll be triggered into survival mode. When in survival mode, we become obsessed with getting our needs met, particularly our needs for security, connection, and, when we feel controlled, freedom. When we're obsessed with getting our needs met, we don't focus on giving what another might need from us; we focus only on getting. We become selfish. Strong, healthy relationships demand that we transcend our primal instinct to self-protect and get our needs met and instead step into the part of ourselves that wants to repair, see the other's perspective, and meet their needs, too. This is our higher self.

When you become stressed and fearful in a relationship, you have an unconscious pattern that you developed to protect yourself from emotional pain. The paradox, though, is that the very thing we do to self-protect in a relationship is usually what sabotages our connection with our partner.

The lower self isn't about feeling our difficult emotions or our fear. The lower self is how we react to our fear. It's our behavior.

What do you do when you're afraid? Do you withhold your love and attention? Do you shut down from your partner? Do you try to make your partner feel insecure, so that you don't feel so insecure yourself? Do you decide not to answer their texts and leave them on read for a couple of hours? Do you give your partner the silent treatment? Are you short and curt in response? Critical or judgmental?

Sometimes the lower self says, *I don't feel like talking right now. I don't want to be bothered by you. I don't want to let you into my heart. I don't want to be open with you. I don't want to be honest with you.*

Punishment is not the path to a healthy, strong relationship. A healthy, strong relationship is not about "getting back" at someone. Part of dissolving the punisher that lives inside of us is understanding why it's there—because we feel hurt, unseen, and insecure. We have to stop manipulating our partners instead of being open and honest in our communication.

We can't punish someone we love without punishing ourselves. All we're doing is creating more distance between ourselves and the other, when really we need to be building bridges to the other by showing up as our higher selves. That's intimacy.

Self-Awareness Is a Relationship Superpower

Self-awareness in a relationship is recognizing when our past hurts and emotional states are controlling our thoughts and behavior. It's being able to see how our insecurities interfere with our ability to connect with our partner and how our energy and behavior impact our loved ones and thus our relationship with them. As you read earlier, romantic relationships are a mirror; whether a relationship is the right one or the wrong one, it will show us where our work is. In other words, when you feel triggered and you start acting like a twelve-year-old, it's all an opportunity to look inward and say, *Okay. This is my stuff. What am I struggling with right now?*

Self-awareness is noticing, *Oh, I'm doing that thing where I'm silently punishing*—and then realizing, *I don't want to be that person. The person I want to be in a relationship is not going to do that.* It's becoming aware of your pattern and then parenting yourself. It's discipline; it's maturity, self-control. We can't expect a child to have self-control; they're not a fully developed being. It is developmentally appropriate for anyone under twenty-five, before their prefrontal cortex is fully developed, to not have control of themselves. But it's no longer developmentally appropriate for adults, with fully formed brains, to have no self-control. At the end of this chapter, I'll address how you can better regulate your emotions.

Self-awareness is a relationship superpower, and everyone has room for improvement when it comes to their own self-awareness. What builds this superpower? Looking in the mirror and being willing to see what is reflected back—the good, the not so good, the pain, and the complexity. It's paying attention to how our energy—positive or negative—affects our environment. Certainly, there are those who have very little to no self-awareness, and those are exactly the people you do not want to be in a relationship with. They are the ones who are ruled by their lower selves. They have no insight into how their actions, behavior, and thinking impact their environment and the people in it. They blame others for their mistakes and avoid taking responsibility; therefore, they have tremendous difficulty in maintaining strong interpersonal relationships. Without insight into themselves, they can't evolve emotionally.

The road to relationship hell is paved with charming people who haven't worked on themselves and therefore are not self-aware—who think love is only something to get, not something to be given.

Overcoming Powerlessness

I recently received a question from a listener of my podcast, *Jillian on Love*:

> *How do you heal from heartbreak when you were mostly the problem? Anxious attachment, jealousy, major insecurity, overly dependent on him, etc. My fiancé broke up with me three months ago after three years together.*

When I responded to the listener, this is what I said: Healing from this kind of heartbreak boils down to self-esteem, self-worth, and self-love. The way that you heal is to say yes to the journey that is beckoning you—a path of learning how to stand on your own two feet emotionally, how to love yourself, and how to meet your needs. Then you can be in a relationship in which you *need* someone because you *love* them (in the words of Erich Fromm), instead of loving them because you need them. Learning how to need someone because you love them, rather than the other way around, is learning the language of love.

And so you need to figure out a way to meet your need for feeling more secure so that you don't feel so powerless in a relationship, because that's really what it boils down to when we have that extreme level of insecurity. Whether we call it anxious attachment, jealousy, feeling overly dependent, or neediness, what we are essentially experiencing is powerlessness, and we don't talk enough about that feeling.

I don't know what that journey is going to be like for you. Maybe it's about getting a new job. Maybe it's about pursuing a specific career path. Maybe it's about learning how to make your own money. Maybe it has to do with you finally pursuing certain dreams that you have been putting on the back burner because you haven't been taking particular risks.

Absolutely it means learning how to communicate, rather than lashing out with clinginess or jealousy. It will include learning how to self-soothe when you feel out of control and how to sit with your discomfort when you're triggered. You're not going to heal overnight.

You need to have someone in your corner, whether it's a therapist or other trusted counsel, who can be the voice of reason when you feel insecure. You should be able to ask this person, *Am I being just overly jealous right now, or is this actually something I should be paying attention to?*

This path involves unlearning everything that has led you to feel deeply incomplete without the presence of a relationship. That's a journey that's worth taking. It is the path that's beckoning you right now. And I want you to be so kind to the part of you who has contributed to the end of this relationship. I know that's going to be hard, but maybe being kinder to yourself is part of what you have to learn.

This is a huge wake-up call. And the call sounds like this: *I am sick and tired of feeling so goddamn powerless in relationships. I've got to figure out what I specifically need to do, what life is asking of me, so I can start to have my own back and feel more whole.*

Looking in the mirror and confronting ourselves takes an enormous amount of courage. The part of us that acts out of character, reacts, and sabotages needs our attention. What is this part of ourselves trying to teach us? What is it illuminating that we have to look at? If you've been in a similar position, and you've sabotaged a relationship, welcome to the club. There's no need to feel ashamed. The point is to study and learn from the experience, so you can choose a better path, and say yes to the journey toward your higher self.

. . . .

PRACTICING THIS TRUTH

Identify Your Inner Saboteur

When you're pissed off, when you're stressed-out, when you feel insecure, when you feel triggered in a relationship or a dating scenario, what do you do, as a form of self-protection?

Do you withhold?

Do you get controlling and possessive?

Do you try to make your partner feel insecure?

Do you pull away?

Do you yell?

Do you get needy?

Do you isolate yourself from your partner?

Do you stop taking care of yourself?

Do you get too comfortable?

Do you stop showing up as the person who showed up at the beginning at the relationship?

Do you get moody and take your moods out on your partner?

Do you need to be right all the time?

How do you withhold your compassion, love, attention, and empathy when you are triggered?

How to Access Your Higher Self

I always envied the cool, calm, and collected—the people who don't easily get swept away by their emotions and who can respond calmly to difficult challenges. I was always a sensitive, reactive type. As a child, I felt all my emotions strongly. If I was frustrated, I would have explosive temper tantrums. When happy, I was extremely gleeful and passionate. When angry, I would scream. Thankfully, my reactivity improved with age. I still feel things intensely, but I have dedicated my life to practicing pausing before I react. I sometimes fail. But I keep practicing.

You access your higher self by first being aware of a disruption to your internal state of being and then, instead of reacting from an agitated inner state, learning to bring yourself back to equilibrium.

The space between trigger and reaction has been studied and taught for centuries by yogic masters, Buddhist monks, and psychologists. The pause is when we learn to use our breath and regulate our nervous systems so that we can choose with greater intention our response to something, rather than being controlled by our initial emotional reactions. As Viktor Frankl, author of *Man's Search for Meaning*, is credited with saying "Between stimulus and response, there is a space. In that space is our power to choose our response. In our response lies our growth and our freedom."

Relationships can be triggering—romantic relationships especially. That's the reason being in a relationship means we must practice being less reactive; the pause before responding to a trigger has the power to save a relationship from our reactivity.

A lot of people sabotage their relationships by being too reactive. Learning how to take a breath, step back, and regulate ourselves so we can respond from a calm place is what makes us a safe partner.

Learning how to be less reactive and more responsive is one of the most important relationship and life skills we can ever work on. Remember it's practice, not perfection. We will not get better at this overnight. It takes a lot of practice.

Learning to become less reactive is like building a muscle. We need to take specific, repetitive actions that train our systems to pause when we feel triggered before responding.

When you're feeling reactive, ungrounded, or just "off," take a moment to pause and check in. Ask yourself: *What am I really feeling right now? Could it be that I'm really sad right now? Could I be tired? Could it be that I'm angry? Could it be that I'm scared?* And then check in with your body, to find where you're feeling tension. Maybe it's your jaw. Maybe it's your lower back. Ask yourself: *If my jaw could speak right now, what would it say? If my back could speak right now, what would it say?* This is a practice of attuning to ourselves emotionally, so that we can begin to let go of any stored tension.

Here are other practices that help:

- Get quiet every day with your eyes closed for about twenty minutes.

- Move your body daily: take long walks, do yoga, stretch, dance, or do whatever exercise makes you feel more grounded.

- Limit sugar and caffeine, and make sure your blood sugar is stable.

- Rest. Stress and exhaustion will make you much more reactive.

- Before you send that text, pick up the phone, or send that email, wait. Take an hour. Take a walk. Then decide. This pause could save your relationship.

Relationships can be triggering. Dating can be triggering. Healing isn't about the absence of triggers. It's training ourselves to observe our minds in the storm of our reactivity and choose another way.

In a relationship, our priority must be connection—maintaining connection and restoring it when it's lost. So what can you start doing today, in any of your relationships, to build a bridge, rather than contribute to a gap between you and the person you care about?

Questions for Reflection

1. Describe your best self in a relationship. How do you want to show up, love, behave, and feel?

2. We all have reactive behavioral patterns that are triggered when we feel unseen, unheard, and underappreciated. What is yours?

Do you cling? Shut down? Do you withhold attention to make the other person feel insecure? Do you do a combination of things? How has this impacted your relationships?

3. The ego says, *I must win this fight. I'm right. My needs are more important than yours. I have to protect myself.* How has *your* ego gotten in the way of your former relationships or your current relationship?

4. How has your need to be validated and loved gotten in the way of you giving validation and love to a partner?

5. We can easily get too comfortable in our relationships and take each other for granted. In what ways have you taken the person you love for granted?

Regardless of what another person is doing or not doing, you want to be able to look in the mirror and say, *I did the best that I could. I showed up. I deepened my self-awareness. I did the work.* That's so important for self-love and self-esteem; having a standard for others is easy, but having a standard for yourself is a game changer.

We can get so caught up in our expectations of others. But the more we commit to showing up as our higher self, in *any* relationship, the more we mature and evolve as people. We become more conscious. We always have the choice to show up as our wiser self or our calmer self. We will have flashes of self-awareness when we realize that we feel fearful, stressed-out, and dysregulated. And that is when we need to say, *I'm going to take a time-out, so that I can come back to this conversation calmly.* Or *I'm going to go work out so that I can calm down.* Or *I'm going to take a nap so that I can relieve some stress. Or I'm going to call a friend. Or I'm going to take a deep breath in and a deep breath out, and take a sip of water, and respond differently.*

We need to have the self-awareness to recognize when we're not treating ourselves or another person we care about the way that we want to. And in that moment, it's time to reevaluate our behavior and self-correct so that we can access our higher selves. Again, you will always have that choice. We all have fear; we all have trauma. Sometimes fear and trauma will indeed get the best of us. This is called being human. Growth requires practicing in small ways, every day, how to respond to our inevitable triggers differently. It is a matter of practice, not perfection.

Regardless of what your partner, lover, date, or family member is doing, at least you can say, *I see where my fear is; I see where my ego is; I'm choosing to behave differently. And when I fail—because I will—I just course correct.*

You Cannot Convince Someone to Love You

You cannot convince someone to love you. This is an absolute, hard truth. It is the law of the land, and there's no escaping it. There is no plan B, what-if, maybe, or *let's see*.

As much as "winning" someone's love has been romanticized in film and literature, love is not something that we win.

When someone you love can't love you back, you have to let them go. Whether it's your partner, your spouse, the father or mother of your child, or just your fuck buddy, you've got to let them go. Period. This is the end of the story, because there *is* no other story when someone no longer wants to be in a relationship with you. There is no other story if someone doesn't want to commit to you.

I know how harsh this truth is, but like all the truths in this book, it will liberate you. I understand how gut-wrenching and disorienting it is to be rejected—especially by someone with whom you've planned a life. When they say, "It's over" or "I'm leaving," you can't try to convince them they don't know what they're doing. Don't negotiate, manipulate, convince, or guilt-trip. Don't try to talk anyone into loving you, paying more attention to you, texting you, calling you. It won't work. It never does. In fact, it will work against you in every way. Even if you somehow manage to convince someone to stay, it won't last. Plus, you'll only be trading in your fear of losing them for the pain of knowing that you had to convince them to stay, which will make you feel more insecure and unloved.

Relationship Status: "It's Complicated"

Stop wasting your life investing in someone who isn't invested in you. If they say they're going through a divorce and aren't ready for a relationship, believe them. If they fear commitment, it's not your problem; don't think it will be different with you, because it won't be. If they have too much trauma to be with you, you can't heal them into being a capable partner. If they just treat you like a fuck buddy, then you better believe that's all you are to them.

The term "situationship" is all over social media, and I love how accurately it describes the complicated "situations" I see countless people engage in. A situationship is an informal romantic/sexual relationship that isn't established and has no signs of becoming a committed relationship. There's nothing wrong with being in something casual, but if one person wants more while the other person doesn't, it's turmoil for the person who wants commitment. They're torturing themselves by agreeing to be someone's maybe.

One of my most important missions is to help people stop chasing those who do not want to be chased. In other words, to accept when someone hasn't chosen them and to choose themselves—their sanity, peace, and dignity—instead. To avoid, at all costs, the "situationship."

Unless two people consciously choose and verbally agree to invest in an uncommitted and undefined connection, it creates a massive imbalance of power, with the person who doesn't want commitment having all the power. The other forfeits theirs by pretending that being casual is okay with them, while they quietly pray that the other person will change their mind and choose them. When we choose to remain connected to someone who can never reciprocate our love, we severely interfere with not only our well-being but our future.

I've seen a lot of people mess up their lives by staying in a situationship.

Over the years, I've received thousands of messages from tortured people who were emotionally attached to someone who didn't share the same feelings and for various reasons didn't want to commit to a relationship. Questions such as "Will he ever leave his wife for me?," "Why does she keep saying she doesn't want a relationship, but then she keeps asking to hang out?," and "How do I get him to choose me?" flood my inbox and DMs daily. Too many people are in situationships because they're too afraid to ask for what they want and are instead preoccupied with figuring out how to get someone to choose them.

Amanda believed that she could heal the damaged men she loved and, as a result, convince them to love her back. When she came to see me, she was thirty-eight years old and very much wanted to get married and have a family. The problem was that instead of dating the available men who asked her out, she was stuck on one guy she'd been dating on and off for more than a year. This man, Peter, was separated with a two-year-old child. Peter claimed that his wife was "toxic" and that he couldn't wait to get divorced. This was what he told Amanda, even though he lived with his wife (though he apparently slept in a separate bedroom).

I already couldn't stand him, but I had to remind myself that Amanda wasn't a victim. She was a grown woman, and it was her responsibility to choose an available, healthy man.

"His wife is really toxic and makes things difficult for him," she told me.

I immediately knew that coaching Amanda was going to require an intervention. If Peter's wife was so "toxic," what did that say about *him*? He'd been in a relationship with her for ten years. Where was his responsibility?

"How so?" I asked, genuinely curious.

"She's just really jealous and doesn't want Peter seeing anyone else. She wants him to stay and threatens to sue for custody of their child if he goes through with the divorce. He's having a really hard time," she replied.

It occurred to me in that moment that Amanda was like many people I've known and worked with throughout the years. She was the healer—otherwise referred to as the coach or therapist—for her lovers. She chose men who needed to be rescued from their difficult circumstances, and she did so by being like Mother Teresa—meaning that she was a constantly available shoulder to cry on and would answer his lonely calls in the middle of the night to give him counsel. Whenever he wanted to see her, she would cancel her plans to be with him. In short, she was the opposite of Peter's "toxic" wife. Amanda was a reliable, loving, steady presence for him. Her unconscious belief was this: *The more I can prove to him that what he needs is a grounded loving woman in his life, the more he will need to be with me, and the faster he will finally leave his wife.*

"Amanda, answer me this: How much time do you spend thinking about Peter and his wife?" I asked, hoping the question would lead to a mini breakthrough.

"It consumes me."

As much as some people want to heal, they're not always ready to make the necessary changes. As much as some people will *say* that they want a loving, committed relationship, their choices say otherwise. Healing takes courage. Breaking patterns takes determination. Not only do we have to want more for ourselves, but we also have to believe we deserve what we want. An uncomfortable truth is that we have to *want* to heal. We have to be willing to reach deep within ourselves and touch the parts that are strong, determined, and certain. I believe we all have the capacity to overcome the relational patterns that are holding us back, but we need others to believe in us and to help show us the way. I believed in Amanda, but my gut told me this wasn't going to be an easy case.

Why We Get into Situationships

One of the top five most common questions I get is about situationships. Every day, I get emails and DMs on Instagram like this one:

> *Dear Jillian,*
>   *I keep finding myself in situationships where I'm the one who wants more. Help!!*

Remember Truth 1? It begins with *you*. If we want to transform our love lives, we have to revolutionize the relationship we have with ourselves. We do so by taking responsibility for our choices and understanding how our fears have interfered with our relationships. We don't simply *find* ourselves in a relationship; we make choices that lead us there. But why do we choose relationships in which we have to work tirelessly to get someone to choose us?

There isn't one answer. I typically find that there are five core reasons we fall into situationships.

Beliefs

A belief is a feeling of certainty about what something means. Our beliefs are created by our experiences and conditioning. The beliefs we develop from painful past experiences are often limiting beliefs— meaning that they are beliefs based on fear that limit us and lead us to poor decision-making. Remember Jade? Jade struggled with low self-worth and didn't *believe* that she was worthy of being truly loved. Consequently, she would chase unavailable men.

Some common limiting beliefs and fears shared by those in situationships:

I'll never meet anyone else.

Available people are boring.

If I just try harder, they'll love me.

If I change, they'll choose me.

I can change them.

I won't meet anyone else I feel this connected to.

I don't want to start over again.

I don't want to feel lonely.

No one wants to date people my age.

There are no good people out there.

The kind of relationship I want doesn't exist.

Conditioning

How many times have you seen someone sacrificing their own needs to sustain a relationship? We are conditioned to believe that we can "win" love. That's what Amanda did when she gave up her dream. Maybe you've seen your parents or your friends approach relationships this way. As I said earlier, the idea that we can win someone's love has been romanticized by fairy tales and films like *The Notebook* and *My Best Friend's Wedding*. But love isn't something that we can force someone to feel or choose.

Loneliness

Wanting to share your life with someone is completely valid. But in today's world of social media, where in theory we are more connected than ever, we are paradoxically also more starved for real connection than ever. Finding community takes effort and doesn't come easily to everyone. Your friends could be in relationships or just busy with their own loves. Context matters, too. For example, the pandemic gave many people a reasonable excuse to engage in relationships that they otherwise never would have in normal circumstances, because of their loneliness.

Boredom

Chronic boredom comes from feeling unfulfilled in our lives. When this happens, we'll seek out a little drama (or a lot) to distract us from the monotony of our lives. On the show *Girls*, Hannah and Marnie are both unfulfilled, directionless, and consequently bored with their lives, so they fill their time with dramatic and complicated relationships. At first glance, you might think that the guys Hannah and Marnie get involved with are the complicated ones, but the truth is, Hannah and Marnie are just as complicated. That makes for a good show, but it's not a good template for healthy relationships. In my work, I witness people who have not yet found real meaning and purpose in their lives fill their time with meaningless relationships as a way to distract themselves. We'll see another case study of this in Truth 8.

Grief

The pain that comes with grieving a loss can be very overwhelming; much as we do in response to boredom, we may seek out difficult relationships so that we can replace our grief with a preoccupation with another person. When we're grieving, sometimes we feel so lost, and all we want is someone to love us. Some people when they're grieving will isolate, but a lot of people will look to fill the hole. To grieve is to mourn the loss of love. Because we feel so lost and because we're not in our right mind (so to speak), we look for love in all the wrong places.

Moving Forward from the Situationship Trap

How could Amanda stay in a faux relationship with a married man for a year? She knew it wasn't healthy for her anymore. But she felt stuck.

Amanda had been emotionally disconnected from her job for years, and when she was thirty-three, she lost her father, her closest confidant. Her father had been a therapist. He was a very patient, loving man who played this role of confidant to his wife, his daughters, and all of his closest friends. Amanda was just like him. Her high degree of patience, empathy, and compassion toward others was one of her greatest strengths. She was a confidant for her close circle of friends and a loving, nurturing big sister to her younger cousins, but she channeled those instincts in the wrong direction when it came to her love life.

Relationships hold many paradoxes, and one of them is that our strengths as a person can also be our fatal flaws if we choose the wrong person to love. Amanda's patience and empathy led her down the road to relationship hell because she lacked the boundaries necessary for a relationship to be a two-way street of love and commitment.

"That sounds really messy, Amanda. So, you've been seeing him for a year without any commitment from him because he can't leave his wife?" I asked, still curious to get all the facts straight.

"Yeah. I know it's not good." She looked sad and defeated.

"Do you want my help in moving on from Peter?" I asked, skeptical that she was ready.

"Yes, I do," she said, unconvincingly.

As a coach, this is when *I* had to reach deep within *myself* to find the patience and compassion that came so easily to Amanda.

Awareness of our patterns is the first step. I explained transparently to Amanda what I believed was her pattern with Peter: that she was trying to quietly convince him she was "The One" by being the caring, patient, and compassionate foil to his wife. I told her that losing her beloved father left a void inside of her that understandably made it hard for her to maintain emotional boundaries with men with whom she felt a connection. And finally, I told her that because she felt deeply unchallenged by her job in sales, she was bored, and her uncertain relationship with Peter provided a distraction from the monotony of her life.

Her eyes widened, and I could see the tears well up. "This makes sense. How do I change this?"

This was the million-dollar question. I was relieved Amanda resonated so strongly with my insights, but I knew that awareness, while it is a critical step toward change, wouldn't be enough.

I worked with Amanda for almost a year. Within the first three months together, she ended things with Peter twice only to take him back again. It was frustrating. Every time I thought she turned a corner, evidenced by her bravely telling Peter what she needed and then walking away when he admitted to not being able to meet her needs, she would cave several weeks later and take him back. I had to surrender to the fact that as much as Amanda knew she should remove Peter from her life, she wasn't yet motivated enough to do it, for good.

I decided to stop focusing on her relationship with Peter and to focus on her relationship with work. Since her father died, Amanda had a dream of one day becoming a therapist, but for financial reasons, she pursued sales to more easily pay her bills and live in the home she wanted to live in. Just when she was considering going back to school to get her master's in psychology, she met Peter. And that is when she forfeited her dream.

This is how most people in situationships ruin their lives. Because these "relationships" are so uncertain, we have to work extra hard to feel safe in them; therefore, we tend to ignore the other parts of our lives in the pursuit of love that isn't fully available to us. Trying to convince someone to choose us becomes our full-time job, and we end up abandoning our personal goals and deepest longings. This is how we self-abandon.

A healthy relationship is a secure one. We choose each other, and when we do, we're not tasked with rejecting ourselves in order to sustain the relationship.

The best way I could support Amanda was to help her return to her goal of becoming a therapist. I couldn't force her to leave Peter, and I couldn't fill the void that existed in her from losing her father. But I could hold her hand as she courageously took the first steps toward a career change that would transform her life for the better. Amanda reached deep inside herself and found the determined, motivated, and confident parts that largely defined who she had been before her father died. As I recommended, she kept her day job while she went back to school so she didn't accrue debt. She studied in the evenings and on the weekends.

A year into her master's program, she had built so much confidence in herself that she finally left Peter for good. This time, it was a much easier decision, because her life felt more meaningful, and she didn't need Peter and his part-time love anymore to distract her. She stopped trying to convince him to love her, and finally, she let go.

Today, Amanda is a therapist and is in a new relationship with another therapist she met in her master's program. This wasn't an overnight process for Amanda. She had many setbacks—mostly caused by her mental resistance to change and facing the unknown. Getting her degree was a huge mountain for her to climb; despite her resistance, she kept going. She was afraid of change, as many of us are, but she didn't give up.

When you think the mountain in front of you is too big to climb, let Amanda's story inspire you to reach down within yourself and find the parts that will no longer settle for less than what you deserve. Let these truths be your constant reminder of how strong you are and your biggest ally as you climb.

Choosing Yourself

To walk away from the person you care about who cannot meet your needs is one of the bravest acts you can do.

We allow the relationships that reflect what we think of ourselves. So we have to love ourselves enough to have boundaries that uphold a standard of how we expect to be treated by others. For some, walking away from a person who isn't capable of or interested in meeting their basic needs for respect, trust, and emotional safety is an act of immense courage. To them, it doesn't feel like they're walking away from less than what they deserve; it feels like they're walking toward the uncertain abyss of singlehood and loneliness again. For some, it will take everything they've got to walk away and finally choose themselves—meaning that they choose their peace and sanity over the chaos of participating in relationships that diminish the quality of their lives.

When you walk away from a person you don't feel good around or safe with, you're not only breaking up with a person, you're breaking up with a pattern. It means you bravely resist your powerful instinct to stay connected and attached in favor of doing what is in your highest good over the long term. When you choose what is best for you rather than remaining in a connection because of your fear of being alone and of starting all over again, you choose yourself. And when you choose yourself, you love yourself. In life, it's rare that you first love yourself and then you decide to choose yourself. It's more a matter of taking that bold step of choosing yourself; in doing so, you will love yourself. The truth is, no amount of connection can ever make up for the anxiety that is guaranteed if we remain in a relationship that we know is not good for our well-being.

Take Action

If you're in a "situationship," it's time to get off the roller coaster. You need and deserve a mutually loving relationship, in which you're both on the same page, all feet in, and clear about where you stand. But you must do your part and stop participating in connections that leave you feeling deprived and famished for more.

After three months of consistently spending time with someone and sleeping together, things should be progressing. You should be integrating into each other's lives. You should be meeting each other's friends. You should be talking about the future. If you're not, then you are headed into a storm of unmet needs and anxiety. And if you, like Amanda, have been in a "complicated" situation with someone for several months or even years, it's time to lay down the boundary. It is not your job to convince someone to love you or commit to you. Your only job is to communicate, leading with truth and vulnerability. So, before you end it, communicate.

Try communicating this:

"I really care about you and I love spending time with you. But I want to be in a committed relationship where we grow together and build a life together. If you're not ready for this, that is okay. But we're not on the same page, and it's best that I move on."

"I love you. But I can't do this anymore. It's not your fault. I have participated in this for too long, and I am now moving on."

Confronting Abandonment: When They Want to Leave

When I first met Olivia, she was devastated. Her husband, Steve, the father of their three children, wanted to separate. The last four years of their relationship had been very tough, and even though they had tried to get help many times with various couples therapists, nothing was working. Olivia was determined to convince him to stay.

During our Zoom session, Olivia appeared frail. Her shoulders were rounded forward and up by her ears, and her lips pursed as she clenched her jaw. It was as if her insides were a pressure cooker waiting to explode at any moment. As I observed her, I was reminded of what it physically felt like when my ex-husband left me.

Olivia's bodily tension was the physical manifestation of her emotional resistance to the end of her marriage. She reminded me of a beaten-down boxer in the ring who has clearly been defeated but won't give up the fight. I was reminded of my own fight when I spent two years trying to save my marriage and how absolutely exhausting and unproductive it was. I felt her pain and knew she had an intense road ahead of her.

My very first instinct was to support Olivia in the letting go of her relationship, but she tried to convince me they just hadn't "tried hard enough."

"He doesn't communicate and I don't think he is making the right decision. He needs someone to knock some sense into him," she said in between anxious tears. "Please, can we all do a session together?"

I agreed to meet with the two of them because I needed to know whether this was a relationship that they *should* fight for (with my help) or let go of.

I'll never forget watching her husband, Steve, squirm uncomfortably as Olivia pleaded with him through her tears to stay. I wanted so badly to jump through the computer screen and rescue Olivia from giving away more of her dignity. When I looked at Steve, I knew he was done and that my initial instinct about their relationship had been confirmed: his decision to leave was final, and their marriage was over.

My work would be to help Olivia let go.

After twenty minutes of watching Olivia beg Steve to stay and "work on their marriage," while Steve defended himself by claiming that he *had* done the work and that separating was the only and best answer to their problems, I interrupted: "Olivia."

She looked at me.

I could feel the tension mount inside me because I knew what I was about to say wasn't going to be easy for Olivia to hear. I took a deep breath. "Olivia, I know this is incredibly difficult. Trust me, I do. But you can't keep trying to convince him to change his mind. What you *can* do is ask him about the pain he feels. You can ask him about how this has been hard for him, too."

I watched Steve as he let out an audible sigh. His body visibly relaxed, and I could see tears start to form in his bloodshot, tired blue eyes.

"I've done everything I could" was all Steve could say.

Breaking up is hard for everyone. Divorce, even when it's amicable, is still an emotional catastrophe that takes time to recover from. No one gets into a relationship wanting it to end, and when we get married, our goal is to stay married until death. The tragedy is that relationships rarely end because of a lack of love. They more commonly end because of a lack of connection that comes from feeling chronically unseen and misunderstood. Couples usually endure hurt feelings, resentment, and insecurity for months or years before one or both people call it quits. People struggle to stay connected to each other because they don't know how to overcome their fears, tell the truth, love selflessly, and love themselves more fully.

I wrote about the nine truths in this book because I know what it feels like to be abandoned and to abandon myself. I've worked with thousands of fearful people trying to heal their love lives. The person who wants to leave a long-term relationship isn't leaving because they don't love their partner. They're much more likely leaving because they don't know any other solution. They're tired. They want to feel better, and moving on feels a lot better than staying. The truth is, we all do the best we can with the level of maturity, awareness, and skill that we have at the time of our relationship. Could things have been different if my ex-husband and I had known these truths and lived them? Sure, maybe. But we didn't, and that's the point. We can only do what we're capable of doing, and the hope is that we grow, learn, and find out exactly how resilient we are.

When we're committed and have built a life with someone, we can't just give up at the first signs of struggle. We do have to fight for the re-lationship. But what does it mean to fight for a relationship? It means we stop the blame game and instead take radical accountability for how we've contributed to the breakdown of the connection. It means we listen to the other person, acknowledge how we haven't been meet-ing each other's needs, and then proactively try to meet those needs.

Sometimes it means recruiting the help of a third party, such as a couples coach or therapist. Sometimes it means patience when the person we love is going through a particularly hard time, and consequently they temporarily cannot contribute emotionally to the relationship at the level they once did.

But it takes two. We can't fight for something that the other has already let go of. We cannot convince someone to change how they feel and stay when they want to leave. We simply cannot bargain with the person who wants to leave. We have to let go. For a relationship to work, both people need to feel free and choose the relationship. When we beg or guilt someone into loving us, we hold them hostage emotionally. And when we do, we end up imprisoning ourselves in a relationship that can never give us what we need.

We also compromise our dignity.

The (Often Unconscious) Ways We Try to Persuade Someone to Love Us

One of the hardest lessons we will face in life is learning to accept when someone's part in our story is over. This is a lesson many of us will try to resist for a long time, until we're left with no choice but to accept it. Until then, people will try really hard, often unconsciously, to win the other person's love again.

Some people will figure out a way to be needed, such as by becoming their partner's "therapist" or "coach," to help them reach their "potential."

Some, like Amanda, will give more—attention, energy, time, gifts, sex, and support—even when they are being given nothing.

Some will beg for the other's love.

Some will use logic to try to persuade the other to see how good they are together.

Some break down, so the other feels too guilty to leave.

Some weaponize their children.

Faced with an impending divorce she didn't want, Olivia pleaded, used logic, and tried to guilt Steve into staying in the marriage. For one month, I committed to being a grounding energy for Olivia and spoke to her multiple times a week. She reflected on her marriage—the fights, the feelings of being lonely and misunderstood—and the truth was that she had been miserable for the past two years. Deep down, a part of her yearned to be free of her relationship with Steve, but understandably, she was afraid of the consequences of being alone and starting all over again as a single mom at fifty.

This ambivalence—longing for the end of the relationship on the one hand, while on the other hand being desperate to keep it—is much more common than we think. Once Olivia recognized her ambivalence toward Steve and her marriage, she was able to stop begging, strategizing, and trying to convince him to keep loving her. To be clear, recognizing her ambivalence didn't take her pain and fear away. Her heart was still broken, and she was still overwhelmed by the road ahead of her. But at least now, she was capable of communicating more productively with Steve about their separation and how to navigate co-parenting. Accepting Steve's decision to leave was the first and most important step in Olivia's heartbreak recovery.

It took Olivia a year to acclimate to her new normal as a single mom and learn how to find a sense of contentment on her own after her divorce. Then she was able to start dating again. Within five months, she met someone, and today she's in a happy relationship. Stories like Olivia's give us hope that there is love after heartbreak.

The truth that you cannot convince someone to love you is meant to inspire you to stop chasing love and to let whoever wants to leave, leave. This truth makes crystal clear that when someone gives you mixed messages, it is not an invitation to please, give, nurture, or manipulate. It is not an invitation to wait to be chosen. It *is* an invitation, however, to stand firm by your own side and not compromise your dignity in any way. I'm here to tell you that there is no force out there that wants to deny you love. You deserve it, and there's plenty of it to go around.

Breaking the Pattern

One of the most profound and impactful decisions I have ever made in my life was to let my husband leave. I had spent two years trying to be enough for him, and I had tried as hard as I could with the limited tools I had at the time to fight for our love, but when he made his decision, I let him leave without a struggle. This is something I feel proud of to this day, because truthfully, letting go made *my* life much easier.

Letting go protected me from repeated rejection. It allowed me to heal.

Whether you're someone who gives all your power away to someone you barely know, or you find yourself in relationships in which you overfunction and jump through hoops to get more love, you *can* break the cycle. And you must break it.

Remember when I listed the most common beliefs shared by those who are in situationships? The following beliefs are the ones most commonly shared among people who are divorcing or ending a long-term relationship. These beliefs are significantly responsible for making us give away our power, and they prevent us from letting go when we need to.

I can't start all over again—it's too exhausting.

I'm forty. I'll never find someone at this age.

It will take so long to find someone else.

Divorced people are pathetic.

If this ends, I'm a failure.

• •

PRACTICING THIS TRUTH

A Meditation

If you've been holding on to someone who cannot love you, a part of you is in survival mode. Losing love feels like losing oxygen, and your fear is understandable. Acknowledge that you're afraid without judging yourself for feeling that way. Then take a comfortable seat and close your eyes. You can rest your hands gently on your thighs, or if it's comfortable, you can rest both hands on your lower abdomen or place one hand on your abdomen and the other across your chest. With your lips gently sealed, take a slow deep breath in through your nose and a slow, longer breath out through your nose. Repeat this for a couple of minutes. Go slow, and if you need to let out a sigh when you exhale, do so. Then, while keeping your eyes closed, remember a time when you felt powerful and full of life. You can go as far back in time as you want to. Try to remember all the details: where you were, what you were doing, the people you were with, what you were wearing, and so on. Focus on the feelings you felt in that moment: the strength, the pride, the joy, the power. Focus on this memory for a few minutes, and when you're ready, go to your next memory when you felt proud of yourself, strong, and full of life. You can do this exercise for as long as you need to, and repeat it every day.

Give to Yourself

It's time to focus on what you need. Start small. Do you need to call a friend? Do you need to speak to a professional? Do you need to work out? Do you need a walk? Do you need more water? Do you need to watch a great movie? Do you need a delicious meal? Give to yourself what you need in this moment. Sounds trite, but giving to ourselves is like building a muscle. If all you've known lately is focusing on the other person and trying to be chosen by them, you've forgotten yourself. So, slowly bring the focus back to you by asking yourself, *What do I need right now?*

Communicate Differently

Notice whether you are falling into the pattern of convincing, begging, or bargaining when your relationship is struggling. Instead, here's what to say for different scenarios of relationships coming to an end. This can be in the form of a conversation or even a letter if saying the words out loud is too hard for you.

When your partner has ended the relationship:

Dear _____, I accept your decision to end our relationship even though it is not what I want. I love you and want to work on us, but I cannot do it alone.

If you suspect a situationship is forming:

My feelings are growing for you and I want a real relationship. I know you are not ready, and that is okay, but I must move on.

When your basic needs are not being met, despite having communicated them, or you're not on the same page about what you both want and expect out of a relationship:

I love you, but I love myself more. I cannot continue like this. I want and deserve more.

Stop Lying to Yourself

When it does finally become clear to you that you cannot convince someone to love you, choose you, or commit to you, you will then tell yourself it's because you're not lovable—that somehow, because this person didn't choose you, you are not worthy of being chosen. Believing this lie that you're not worthy is what keeps you trapped in the cycle of chasing the unavailable. Remember Amanda and Olivia? It had nothing to do with Amanda that Peter didn't "choose" her. He couldn't untether himself from his wife. Olivia and Steve had problems that left them both feeling disconnected. More often than not, people end marriages because they want an end to their pain. Stop telling yourself you're not good enough.

Make a Promise to Yourself

Stop scheduling more talks, and stop writing the other person letters trying to convince them of the rarity of your connection and how good you are together. If someone you are in a relationship with (or you have been consistently spending time with for at least three months) is unsure about you—unsure whether they want things to progress with you or whether they love you—don't try to please them into loving you. Don't try to heal them into loving you. Stop giving more and trying *to be* more so that the person chooses you. You can't torture yourself anymore being someone's maybe or convenience. It's time to write a manifesto stating a promise to yourself. I suggest writing it and putting it up somewhere where you can read it every day. Write it in a way that feels authentic to you. Here's an example:

I promise to never again wait to be chosen. I will instead decide who is good for ME and invest in a relationship only when our feelings are mutual and our goals are aligned.

I promise that I will never accept part-time love from anyone ever again. Instead of accepting crumbs of attention, I will communicate what I want and how I feel, leading with the truth. If the other person is not on the same page as me—no matter the reason—I will accept this and walk away.

I promise to do what I can to work on my relationship, but I cannot do that alone, and I refuse to do it alone. If my partner wants to exit the relationship, I will be honest about my pain and my wish for things to be different, but I will let them leave if that is what they want.

I promise to never again chase unavailable, aloof, or simply not-right-for-me people and then tell myself the story that I'm always rejected and not good enough to be chosen. I am responsible for my choices, and if I am repeatedly being rejected, it is my duty to examine why without telling myself it is because I am not worthy.

Someone's love is never something you should have to earn. For a relationship to work, feelings need to be reciprocated. The timing has to be right for both people. You cannot make a relationship work when one person wants to leave, or one person doesn't have the same feelings, or one person isn't in a position in their life to commit. If we don't accept that reality, we give someone else enormous power over our lives.

Letting go of the dream of what could have been with someone, or letting go of someone you've spent years of your life with, is one of the most painful experiences of all. If rejection and unrequited love weren't so painful, there wouldn't be so many songs written about that pain. It explains Taylor Swift's whole career!

Sometimes the person we love will stop loving us. Sometimes the person we want so badly doesn't want us as badly in return.

As someone who has survived tremendous heartbreak and gone on to coach thousands of people through their heartbreak recovery, I know that moving on from unrequited love is one of the most treacherous mountains to climb. I also know that when someone wants to leave, you have to let them leave and trust that your destiny is no longer tied to this person.

—

No One Is Coming to Save You

Everyone longs for wholeness and has emotional gaps inside of them. And everyone thinks that the right partner will make them happy. And the right partner probably will—in the beginning. But we can't depend on someone else to make us happy all the time.

When we depend on another flawed human being to make us happy, our dependence will paradoxically lead to unhappiness. Another person—no matter how well suited for us—can't possibly make us feel secure and happy all the time. And once we realize the other person's limitations, we will be crushed by the weight of our failed expectations. We'll feel let down, hurt, and in many cases, as we saw with Lauren in Truth 6, angry at our partner for not magically pulling us out of our negativity.

The main reason anyone would want to be in a relationship is to magnify positive emotion—to feel more joy, excitement, and connection. As we exit the falling-in-love stage and enter the committed stage of a relationship, however, we often face a rude awakening: our problems are still there and we have to deal with them. The emptiness we felt before the relationship is still there. The job we don't like is still our job. The anxiety we struggle with returns after a brief hiatus. And we discover that the person we thought was perfect is actually just as flawed as we are.

The truth is this: A relationship is meant to make us *happier*, not happy. To better the quality of our lives, not rescue us from our lives. To magnify positive emotion, not protect us from negative emotion. There's no question that the love and companionship of a partner should make your road a little easier to walk. But no one can walk your path but you.

We need to feel secure in our relationship, but our lover cannot be the only source of our security.

We need to feel connected to and loved by our partner, but our relationship cannot be the only source of connection and love we feel.

We need to feel enough for our lover, but it won't be enough if *we* don't feel enough on our own.

We need to feel happy in our relationship, but a significant other cannot consistently make us happy when we haven't learned how to access joy on our own.

The expectation that the "right person" will cure our unhappiness is not a conscious one. Most people, when they get into a relationship, don't recognize that subconsciously they are thinking, *Oh good, now I don't have to do anything because my partner and our love will make everything better.* But this narrative runs deep, because we've been influenced for centuries by romance novels and more recently by romantic comedies to believe that love saves the day. This is the misconception of "happily ever after." Every single person I have ever worked with and have ever known has had this (unconscious) belief.

The Romantic

Casey was one of the first clients I ever worked with.

Casey was a twenty-nine-year-old California native who loved yoga, psychology, and personal development. Her dream since she was a little girl had been to get married and have a family. As an only child with divorced parents, Casey spent much of her childhood playing for hours alone with her toys and daydreaming about one day falling in love with a tall, handsome knight and raising a family. Casey was a deep-feeling child with a rich inner world. She spoke frequently to her "pretend friend," would draw different-colored hearts in her coloring book, loved to play dress-up in her mother's clothes, and would pretend she was a mommy, prancing around the house with her three dolls in a stroller. In her teenage years, she spent hours listening to music about lost love, reading Jane Austen and Emily Brontë, and watching romantic comedies and dramedies.

As someone who grew up with two older sisters in the concrete jungle of Manhattan, and who started clubbing at fifteen, on the surface my life looked completely different from Casey's. And yet, I had never related to a client as much as I did to Casey. I, too, was a sensitive child with a rich inner world that included a pretend friend. I played alone for hours at a time, dressed up in my mother's clothes, and daydreamed about love and my knight in shining armor.

When I meet with a new client, I always ask about their former relationships to give me insight into their patterns as well as the type of people they're attracted to. Casey's relationship history didn't surprise me. There was her five-month situationship with Chris, the charismatic, highly intelligent, cocaine-addicted, narcissistic lothario whom Casey found very seductive. When Casey met him, she'd been single for more than a year, which was incredibly hard for a person who had spent most of her life daydreaming about being in love with her knight. Being single for Casey was like being stuck in purgatory. It was a waiting game, and she could never truly feel content without a man in her life. This chronic discontentment while being single put Casey at a massive disadvantage in the dating world. Because she was deeply lonely and thirsty for male attention, she was vulnerable to being seduced by sly charmers like Chris. Chris preyed on women just like Casey and knew exactly how to seduce them. He showered her with praise and compliments, and he took her to lavish dinners and exciting weekend getaways to five-star resorts in the Caribbean. They also had long philosophical conversations about the meaning of life—conversations that Casey loved and that made her feel deeply connected to Chris.

Unfortunately, though, as is the case with cocaine-addicted narcissistic lotharios, he quickly became unreliable and was far more interested in partying and having sex than he was in building a life with someone. One night, when he was supposed to pick her up to go on a date, he never showed up. Despite her efforts to reach him, he stopped responding to her texts and calls.

Before that, there was Tim. Tim was the nurturing type and was twenty-five years older than Casey; he was a safe, fatherly figure to her. A big issue was that he had two kids in their early twenties and didn't want more children. Casey, even though she absolutely wanted children, still continued to see Tim, hoping he'd change his mind over time. Unsurprisingly, he didn't, but Casey remained with him for a year until he finally did the right thing and ended it with her so she could fulfill her dream of becoming a mom one day.

Then there was Eric. Eric was everything Casey had wanted since she was a little girl: he was tall, handsome, from a good family, and financially secure, and he wanted children.

Jackpot.

Eric was perfect on paper, but he and Casey were intrinsically incompatible. He loved the outdoors and preferred to spend weekends hiking and biking. A perfect weekend away for him was to go camping, even in the wintry cold months. Casey disliked the outdoors and hated camping. She preferred to spend her free time at museums and yoga studios, and her perfect weekend getaway was at a beach with visits to a spa for massages. Casey loved to have deep philosophical conversations about God, spirituality, and the meaning of life. Eric was an atheist. According to Casey, Eric didn't understand her sense of humor, and his felt offensive to her.

Casey longed to quit her job in advertising and become a full-time mother. Eric wanted a wife who worked, even after having kids.

Despite being terribly mismatched, they stayed together for almost two years, frequently arguing. Eric eventually broke up with Casey, and even though she wasn't fulfilled in their relationship, she was devastated.

That was when she came to see me.

Casey was a romantic who was in love with love, and she had been endlessly waiting since she was seven years old for her knight to rescue her. The biggest problem with romantics who are in love with love is that they struggle to find meaning in life while single, so they often find themselves trapped in unsatisfying, totally misaligned relationships—because almost anything feels better than being single and loveless.

This extreme aversion to being without a partner caused Casey to be easily seduced by anyone who appeared to have the potential to be her knight. This is how romantics give their power away: instead of being discerning and patient, they victimize themselves by remaining in relationships with the wrong people.

Chris seduced her with his charisma and was the classic "love-bomber." He showered her with fancy dinners, praise, and great conversations. This treatment would be intriguing for most women; however, to the hopeless romantic who feels empty when single, it is the ultimate seduction.

Tim's grounded, safe, fatherly energy attracted Casey to him. As a child of divorced parents whose father had moved out when she was six years old, Casey found the older, nurturing man, who made her feel secure, alluring, even though they were in completely different life stages and Tim would never meet her need to have a family.

Eric was the man Casey had always dreamed of. He was the representation of her ideal: tall, handsome, smart, wealthy, and family-oriented. Casey, intoxicated by the dream of what life with Eric would be, was unable to take a sober look at the myriad ways they were deeply incompatible and, therefore, wrong for each other. His ending their relationship pushed Casey to the edge of her anxiety. She was now terrified she would be alone forever.

As she recounted these three relationships to me, I could see her sadness and her frustration. She pulled her long, blond hair back in a ponytail, as many of us do when we get hot from the rising up of intense emotions. Her eyebrows furrowed, and her green eyes looked contracted and tense.

"I'm so frustrated, Jillian. I feel like all these men failed me, and now I'm alone."

Somehow, I felt comfortable being super direct with her. It must have been because I knew she valued introspection and being challenged—so I took a chance and told it like it was.

"I understand how you feel," I said compassionately. "But—these men didn't really fail you, Casey. They just were totally wrong for you, and you didn't want to see the red flags. You see, there is no one coming to save you, Casey. There is no knight in shining armor coming to sweep you away into the sunset and live happily ever after with you. He doesn't exist. Love doesn't save the day—in fact, love isn't even enough to sustain a relationship for the long term."

All of a sudden, I felt as though I was telling a five-year-old that Santa Claus doesn't exist. Her eyes widened.

Fuck. I had to tell her my most important point quickly, before I crushed her dream entirely.

"But," I continued, "what *does* exist is someone you can cocreate your life with. Someone you can collaborate with as you take on life's challenges and whose back you can have when they go through hard times, and vice versa. Someone with whom you can enjoy your life and do fun things. But that person is not coming into your life to rescue you, Casey, because you don't need to be rescued. You've been deluded, as many of us have been, into believing that your life is meaningless if you're single. It's not. It doesn't have to be that way. I am in full support of you being in a relationship, but not any relationship—the right one for you. And I'm not in support of you suffering until you meet the right person."

Her body significantly relaxed, and she looked intrigued. I relaxed, too, relieved that I may have gotten through to her.

Then came the question I always get:

"But *how*? How can I be okay with being alone and how do I meet the man I will marry?"

"Well, I am sorry to say, it starts with being alone," I said, breaking the bad news. "But I want to help you appreciate it more."

The following six months with Casey were illuminating and, to this day, continue to have a powerful influence on my beliefs and teaching. Working with her affirmed to me that people, when they want to, can change. They can overcome deep-seated beliefs and conditioning and make different decisions that support their lives. Because she was among the first twenty people I had ever coached, I was nervous that what I wanted her to do wouldn't work. I was worried that she would resist my suggestions every step of the way and then tell me that I couldn't help her. She had been in therapy before and had worked briefly with a dating coach. What if I couldn't help her? What if I failed her like the men of her past and I, just like them, couldn't rescue her?

To some professionals, Casey would have been considered "a love addict" or "codependent," and if I'm honest, when I look back, I can see some of those qualities in her. But, when I worked with her, I saw so much more in Casey. I didn't see a woman addicted to love; I saw a woman who was conditioned to believe that she needed to be saved from the monotony of her life by the love of a man. I saw a woman who had depth and an inner strength that she wasn't aware of yet. I didn't see her as broken. I only saw potential. And I was very, very lucky that she was willing to do things differently.

This is how I helped her: I asked Casey to make the conscious choice to not date for six months. She had a supportive friend group, but a few of them were in relationships, which made her feel more anxious about being single. Consequently, she spent more time with her single friends, commiserating over food and drinks about how hard the dating world was and sharing nightmare dating stories. Basically, she and her friends were feeding one another's fears. I suggested she start doing activities with her friends that had nothing to do with men or dating, such as going to see art, listening to live music, going on hikes, going to a yoga class, or trying surfing together. She and her friends needed to have more interesting and exciting experiences together that weren't centered around cruising for men or even talking about them. I then tasked her to spend more time with her coupled friends and their partners. This time, I told her, instead of being discouraged by the fact that they were in relationships and she wasn't, she needed to observe them and take note of what she admired about their relationships, as well as what didn't feel right for her. She needed to learn from them, not waste her time being jealous of them.

I wanted Casey to spend more time with her father. Because he moved out when she was very young, his daily physical absence had left an emotional scar inside Casey. She loved her father, and although she spoke to him a couple of times a week, she didn't see him more than once a month. When she agreed to spend more quality time with him, I was pleased and relieved. Fortifying her relationship with her father was paramount to healing the old wound of his absence from her childhood home.

On the days she felt lonely and sad and her mind became a battlefield of what-ifs, self-pity, and doubt, I asked that Casey regulate her emotional states by going for a long walk, calling a good friend, listening to uplifting music, or watching an uplifting movie. I also asked that she write down all her fears and send them to me. For months, I received her fearful texts—some of which were as long as letters— almost every day. And then they became scarcer and scarcer.

After five months of Casey filling her weekends with activities she usually reserved for when she was seeing someone, and spending more time with couples and taking notes, she told me something that completely floored me.

"I think I'm going to go to Italy this summer—alone."

I almost choked on the water I had just taken a sip of. "Really? Alone?" I asked curiously.

"Yeah. I've always wanted to go. I mean, to be honest, I've always dreamed of going to Italy with a boyfriend, but none of them wanted to go! So, I guess I'll be my own best friend and take my single ass to Italy!"

"What about going with a friend?" I asked, testing the waters.

"I thought about asking someone—but I always wanted to do this, Jillian, and was too afraid. I'm still scared, but I'm also excited. I kind of can't wait." Casey smiled mischievously.

I looked at Casey and saw a different woman. I saw a woman who was saving herself. I smiled back and wished I could hug her.

The Rescuer

Just as many women have been conditioned to buy into the myth that a knight in shining armor will rescue them with his love, many men have been conditioned to believe that they need to be the hero who rescues the vulnerable damsel in order to feel worthy of love. These men tend to gravitate toward people who feel broken in some way and therefore need them. This leads to a complicated and unsatisfying relationship because even though the man might feel important and needed, he will struggle to feel truly connected to his partner. At some point he recognizes he can't save his partner from their brokenness. He can't actually fill their emotional voids. He might stay in the relationship, however, tortured by his inability to transform himself into the knight in shining armor.

Women play the role of rescuer, too. Remember Amanda from Truth 7? She unconsciously tried to therapize Peter out of his toxic marriage. Those of us who have a large degree of empathy—who become teachers, healers, therapists, and coaches—love to help people. We see the potential in everyone, and we've derived a large part of our significance in life from being able to help others reach what's possible for them. In a relationship, seeing someone's potential is a beautiful thing, and to be honest, we *will* sometimes be our partner's coach, and that is okay. It's when we secretly wish they would change, instead of fully accepting who they legitimately are today, that we get ourselves into trouble. Also, when we focus only on another's growth, healing, and change, we end up ignoring our own needs and potential. We become self-abandoning and ultimately resentful, exhausted, and miserable.

To be clear, when we're in a relationship, of course we will be emotionally invested in each other. We will need each other's compassion and support. Be an ally to your partner. Be their greatest supporter and fan. But don't turn them into a project, because ultimately their problems are not yours to solve.

Never date someone you need to heal or reform. You need a partner, not a patient. But always remember, it's not about them—it's about you breaking your pattern of thinking that you can change someone or be the inspiration for their transformation. No matter how hard you try, you cannot compete with someone's childhood. If they haven't addressed their pain, you cannot do it for them.

The following are some clues that you have a pattern of being a fixer or a rescuer in your relationships:

- You choose partners who have a lot of work to do on themselves. They could be addicts or those who have a lot of unprocessed and unaddressed trauma.

- You're drawn to "potential." Even though the person is stuck and unmotivated to change, you stick around because you see so much in them.

- You choose people who are going through a particularly challenging time in their lives—such as a divorce or the death of a loved one.

- You often feel like your partner's parent, teacher, or therapist.

- You choose partners who have a troubling track record in relationships (cheating, lying, inability to open up, never had a relationship that lasted longer than a few months), and yet you justify their behavior and think it will be different with *you*.

- You play the role of a spiritual teacher in your relationship. You want to help the other person, so you expose them as much as possible to all your practices, such as yoga, meditation, and eating well. You are the grounded force in their life and give them advice all the time.

- You tend to get controlling in your relationships, trying to force your partner to break habits and change.

The tools you need to break this pattern are all outlined in this chapter. When we make reaching our own potential important to us, we no longer will use relationships as a distraction. When we learn to save ourselves, we will stop needing to save others.

Using a Relationship to Escape Ourselves

When our lives feel directionless, we can easily use a relationship as an excuse to avoid focusing on steering our lives back on track. When our lives lack the adventure and novelty of new experiences, we can easily use a relationship to distract us from what's missing in our lives.

Remember Adam from Truth 3, who struggled with realizing that his relationship with his influencer girlfriend, Andrea, was rooted more in chemistry than in real love? Although I wanted to help Adam pick more down-to-earth, family-oriented women with better values than his ex, Wellness Barbie, what concerned me most about Adam was that he was a bit lost and lacked the ambition necessary to find his purpose in life.

I worked with Adam for a year and a half, helping him to find greater meaning in his life. He worked in pharmaceutical sales but wasn't emotionally connected to his work. He loved playing sports but made excuses about not having time to play them. He loved to travel, and even though he had more than enough financial resources to travel anywhere he wanted to go, he rarely left his zip code. Adam spent most of his time alone, in isolation, even though he had a good, supportive friend group who invited him out to dinner and events weekly. Adam was completely addicted to certainty. He took no risks and lived a very controlled life in which every day looked and felt exactly like the last.

"I feel very unfulfilled," he told me bluntly during a call.

"I know, Adam. How could you not?" I answered, also bluntly.

During that very same call, Adam told me that he met someone named Naomi. This was about five months after the wellness influencer broke up with him. I was relieved to hear that our work in reforming his picker had paid off! Naomi didn't resemble his ex in any way. Not only did she look completely different, but she seemed to have stronger values, too. She didn't date a lot and was looking for a serious relationship that would evolve into marriage and kids. She was Jewish, which Adam had recently discovered was important to him since he wanted to raise his kids in the Jewish faith. She was a hard worker and supported herself with her job at a small tech company. She also had a rich, full social life and prioritized spending quality time with her friends trying new things. She loved to travel. Every weekend in Naomi's world was filled with new experiences. She had everything Adam was missing from his life.

Sometimes when we're stuck in life, held back by our fears and indecision and unable to create necessary change, we'll get into a relationship and feel inspired by the other person to expand ourselves. But much more commonly, we'll remain the same and over-rely on our partner to save us from our discontent. This is what Adam did. He focused only on Naomi. Instead of making plans with his friends, he would always wait to see when she was available. When she had plans with her own friends, he would just wait on his couch for her to call when she got home. Adam was either *with* Naomi or *waiting* for Naomi. He was *always* available, and I don't mean emotionally. He didn't have a life that preoccupied his attention, so from the very beginning, he made his relationship with Naomi the focal point of his life.

Adam and Naomi were in a relationship for ten months, until she broke up with him.

The success of a romantic relationship is largely determined by two choices: the person we choose and how we decide to show up. Adam had made significant progress in choosing a woman like Naomi, especially compared to his last choice. But the hard truth is, if we don't look inside ourselves and take measures to fill our emotional voids, we will put too much pressure on a relationship to fill them for us. We will, in essence, expect our lover to save us.

Adam was alienated from himself. He valued connection but didn't take the time to connect with peers. He valued growth but refused to step outside his comfort zone. He hated his job but resisted exploring another, more inspiring job. His life, as he admitted, was unfulfilling, and he unconsciously used Naomi to escape from it.

Ultimately, Adam's world was too small for Naomi, and she felt too much pressure to be his everything—so she ended their relationship.

Before you panic over the size of your own world, please know that Adam's story isn't meant to scare you or make you paranoid. You don't have to be traveling the world, have a huge friend group, or be in constant pursuit of new experiences to have a strong, long-lasting relationship. But you *do* have to have a life that matters to you. The way we live our lives won't align with everyone we're attracted to, but we will be less attractive if we don't live it intentionally.

I felt bad that Adam was hurting from his split with Naomi, as I would feel for anyone with a broken heart. But I also knew he needed this to happen. Naomi had no interest in rescuing Adam, and that was a good thing. He had to learn how to save himself.

Unrealistic Expectations

Most people have the belief that their partner is supposed to make them happy. For many, this is an unconscious belief, and for others, it's more conscious.

"He isn't making me happy!" many will complain. Or "I don't think she makes me happy." If we are ambivalent about our relationship, we'll ask ourselves, *Do they make me happy?* Or we will be asked by others, especially family members, "Does this person make you happy?" And when we're asked, we'll search our minds for evidence that we're happy. If we're not, we might then think the other has failed us in some way and become resentful.

Don't get me wrong. I think we should be adding to each other's lives—and rather significantly, too. Life should overall be better because of your relationship. Many of us know how a bad relationship greatly reduces the quality of our lives, and I don't recommend staying in bad relationships. But expecting a relationship to add value to our lives is not the same thing as placing on our partner the heavy burden of responsibility for our happiness.

If you recall Lauren in Truth 6, she had a pattern of becoming very moody in her relationships after the honeymoon phase. She would then blame her partners for not putting up with her moodiness better and for not loving her in spite of it. On top of that, instead of being responsible for her emotional states and learning how to soothe herself when she was stressed, she expected her partners to soothe her, very much the way a parent would soothe a child.

You might think Lauren is a unique case, but she's not.

She's you. And she's me.

Inside all of us is a child who yearns to be taken care of. We secretly crave a partner who will meet all of our emotional needs, all of the time. We want, and often expect, to be loved even when we're not being loving to our partner. Ultimately, we expect that the love of a partner will solve all our existential crises or at least make us forget that they exist. I know, personally, sometimes I really wish someone would rescue me from my problems and distract me from my mind when it's a battlefield of overthinking and negativity. Sometimes, I really wish someone would save me from my unhappiness, but I know that no one is responsible for my happiness but me. This is an absolute truth.

My pursuit of happiness began when I started studying yoga almost twenty-five years ago. I had always used physical movement to calm my mind. For me, exercise was never about sculpting my body to look a certain way; it was survival. If I couldn't at least take a walk, I'd easily get restless and unhappy. But when I discovered yoga, I discovered the key to my internal peace.

The physical part of a yoga practice, otherwise known as hatha yoga or yoga asana, was designed with one goal: quiet the mind so that you can see, feel, and know the love and peace that already exists within you. With consistent, dedicated practice aligning your breath with specific postures, you will ultimately balance your mind, emotions, and nervous system.

When we are in balance, we are at peace. And when we're at peace, we are not searching for happiness in a relationship, money, food, drugs, or anything we can purchase. We learn that what we want to feel comes from within. We just have to remove all the muck of our overactive minds to access it.

Forget Happiness, We Need Purpose

When my life fell apart in 2014, I rebuilt it by pursuing the things that gave my life a sense of purpose. With everything going on, I was depressed, and it simply wasn't possible for me to "just be happy." But because my life had been so consumed with saving my marriage for the past two years, I was finally able to focus on myself. In doing so, I learned two life-changing lessons: First, focusing on the things that gave me a sense of peace was medicine for my mental health.

And second, instead of trying to be happy, I had to figure out what was going to make my life feel meaningful that had nothing to do with a romantic relationship. I did this by pouring whatever energy I had into learning a new craft—becoming a relationship coach.

Everyone needs to feel their life has meaning to feel connected to themselves. In fact, we transform our relationship with ourselves when we find greater purpose for our lives.

Everyone has a deep-seated need to achieve mastery in *something*, to intentionally engage with their life by pursuing the things that matter to them. And a hard but necessary truth is that most of us are turned off by someone who has no direction in life.

Purpose looks different for everyone, and it often isn't grand, glamorous, or based on monetary achievement. In fact, there are many people who have achieved a lot but still feel lost, because they don't feel emotionally connected to the work that they do. A sense of purpose comes from doing things in life that feel meaningful to us, even if they are challenging. For example, some people have found their path in helping the sick and elderly pass away as peacefully as possible by being their nurse either in their homes or in a hospice facility. This is not an easy job. Many of these practitioners feel connected to their patients, and all of them will witness countless strangers break down with grief. Although they have to spend so much time around sadness and grief, being able to help someone transition from living to dying feels incredibly meaningful and important to these practitioners.

You certainly do not have to be a saint who helps people die more peacefully! But after working with several thousand people in trying to help them better their lives, I've learned a powerful lesson about the role of purpose in romantic relationships: it's important to have some sort of mission outside of your relationship and outside of your role as a partner, spouse, and a parent. By "mission," what I mean is something you actively pursue that isn't just a hobby (though I do support having hobbies) and that motivates you and gives you a sense of direction in life. This could be your work—regardless of what that work is—or it could be a special project of some sort. Even women I know who are mothers have expressed the need, at some point in their lives, for a meaningful pursuit that goes beyond nurturing their children.

. . . .

PRACTICING THIS TRUTH

Become Your Own Hero

In order to have the healthy, secure, loving relationship you desire, you have to be radically honest with yourself. You have to ask yourself tough questions: for example, *How many times have I wanted a partner to be different so that I could feel better?* or *How many times have I expected perfection from a partner?* If you're really being honest, how much have you relied on a partner to rescue you from the battlefield of your mind and heal you from your pain?

Becoming your own hero isn't about becoming so tough and independent that you don't need anyone but yourself. I don't want you to ever feel ashamed of wanting a relationship or concerned because you sometimes feel lonely and deprived of attention, praise, and touch. Becoming your own hero is learning how to fill the emotional gaps that live inside of you on any given day, week, or year, without expecting a romantic partner to do it all for you.

I believe in relationships. I believe that when we feel so loved by someone, it helps accelerate our healing. But, as you now know, it begins with us. And life is far better when we know how to be our own savior.

By being our own hero, we cultivate our most primal, core need from within: certainty. Life can be hard and filled with many circumstances that are completely out of our control, and it's easy to feel victimized by those circumstances. When we learn how to access internal contentment all on our own, we become a force to be reckoned with. We become the hero, goddess, warrior, and champion of our story.

How to Make Your Life More Meaningful, Fill Your Inner Voids, and Transform Yourself into Your Own Savior

This chapter is about finding meaning and not relying on a partner to give us meaning. It is also about how to feel content beyond the context of a romantic relationship. The practices in Truth 4 are also worth revisiting.

1. Find joy in the little things.

If we need our day to be perfectly charming, easy, sunny, and inspiring to feel "happy," we will be miserable. Finding joy in the little things is about training ourselves to see more things we can be grateful for. Negativity is a habit, and the only way to break it is to make it easier to feel good.

Try this: On a piece of paper, write down "I feel good when I _____." Then make a list of easily achievable things to feel good about. For example, *I feel good because I woke up this morning. I feel good when I take a walk. I feel good when I call a friend. I feel good when I see an animal.*

For one month, practice appreciating the little things. If it's rain-ing and you don't like the rain—you prefer sun—then try to find something that you can appreciate about the rain. Maybe you like the smell of rain. Maybe there's been a drought. Maybe you can use the rain as an excuse to rest.

2. Move your body—often.

If you can move your body, that is something to celebrate. Research has shown that physical exercise and movement reduce stress, anxiety, and depression.

One size doesn't fit all when it comes to exercise, as everyone has different needs and physical capacity. Here are some suggestions:

- For feeling grounded and strong: lifting weights
- For letting go of stuck emotions: dancing or yoga
- For ease on your joints and increasing focus: swimming or yoga
- For creativity and calming an overactive mind and nervous system: walking or hiking
- For overall health: stretching

One thing that I believe to be medicine and easily attainable for most people is stretching. Stretch every single day, and take some deep breaths when you do.

Another way to change your physiology is through working with a body worker you trust. This may not be possible for you, so please don't worry if it's not. The other suggestions in this section are enough. If you can work with someone, however, I suggest working with a person who is skilled in deep myofascial release or acupuncture. Although there is scientific debate about whether our bodies store negative emotions and trauma, it is my firm belief that they do. The bestselling book *The Body Keeps the Score* by Bessel van der Kolk is a compelling work about how trauma is stored in our bodies. It is my experience that when we release tension deeply lodged in our tissues, we will simultaneously experience a release of suppressed emotions that may have been contributing to a decline in our well-being.

3. **Cultivate multiple sources of connection.**

When a partner becomes the only source of our love, we will suffer. Simply put, it is too much to expect a partner to be everything to us. We need other friends to confide in and talk to about different subjects. We need hobbies that are our own; we need family members, friends, community, or a mentor that we can rely on, too.

Have you ever started a relationship and stopped seeing your friends? Or stopped doing the things you love? Or stopped spending time with family? This is common for many, and I've even been there. But it's a mistake.

Take the time now to invest in the important people in your life.

If you're lacking community, here are some suggestions for finding it:

- Volunteer your time somewhere where there are like-minded people who share a common interest or mission.
- Join a gym or yoga studio. Go regularly.
- Join a religious or spiritual center.
- Join an online group in which everyone shares a common goal.
- Join a neighborhood sports team.
- Host a potluck dinner for neighbors.

4. Give back in some way.

If you want to feel more whole, contributing your time and energy to something outside of yourself is necessary. We can't always be happy. Grief and struggle are part of the human condition. But we learn to save ourselves when we pursue fulfillment instead of "happiness." Giving back is a tragically overlooked and incredibly fast way out of the messiness of our minds and into the clarity of our hearts. The truth is, giving to something outside of ourselves is a nonnegotiable path to greater fulfillment in life. It doesn't matter whether you're contributing to a cause, a person, a client, a student, or an animal.

5. The paradox of healing: let go and have fun.

I realize that you may already be adventurous, and you may have mastered the art of having a good time. However, if you prioritize security, routine, and control, then I can bet that you would benefit from letting go and learning how to have more fun. When we value certainty and safety disproportionately higher than anything else, we tend to walk around with a lot of tension, both physically and mentally. Our lives become organized around how we can maintain the most control. If this is you, I understand you. I've been you. The truth, though, is that to enjoy life, we have to feel alive inside. To feel alive, we can't play it safe all the time. This is one of the greatest paradoxes of healing: clinging to certainty is often a response to having had to deal with too much *uncertainty* in our past. And yet, giving ourselves the permission to do the things that light us up is what will ultimately heal us.

I'm not suggesting that you ignore your responsibilities in life or quit the routines that keep you healthy and mentally stable. But I am suggesting that you make some changes.

Try this: Write down everything that you love to do—even if you haven't done these things in ages or can justify why you should not do them. Some examples could be traveling, going to concerts or listening to live music, dancing, singing, going out with friends, roller coasters, and so on. Just get down as much as you can. The reason you love to do these things is that they touch a deep part of you—a part that is unburdened by trauma, fear, worry, and rules. You love these activities because they make you feel alive. For one month, do at least one thing on your list every week. You can start slow and gradually add to your week when you start to acclimate. If you feel ready to make a bigger leap right away, go ahead!

6. Build financial freedom.

It's important to have your own money so that you're not financially dependent on someone else. In today's world, for example, it's becoming less and less common for women to be entirely financially dependent on their spouses. This is a good thing. Nonetheless, countless people still feel trapped in their long-term relationships because they're unable to financially support themselves. As someone who was in a similar position when I was married, I can tell you that few things are as scary—not to mention incredibly demoralizing—as facing divorce unable to take care of yourself financially. If you are someone who depends on partners for your finances, it's time to take steps toward your financial freedom.

Here are some suggestions:

- People are funny with money. Most have many psychological

barriers to making a good income. Beliefs such as *I'm not an earner, I don't understand money, I'm not smart enough to make money,* and *money doesn't grow on trees* hold people back from financial independence. You must identify the limiting beliefs you have about money and your ability to earn it. There are books that can help you, too. Jen Sincero's *You Are a Badass at Making Money* is a good resource for challenging those beliefs. Tony Robbins's *Money: Master the Game* is excellent for teaching you how to invest your money (even the smallest amount) wisely so that you can become wealthy.

- Study a craft and develop skills. In Truth 4, I spoke to how important it is to follow the clues of your younger self's interests and pursue the things that you have an emotional connection to or that you're curious about. You must be determined. Don't expect to become an expert overnight—just begin.

- Get a job, or start monetizing your skills. In today's world, people don't even have to leave their home to work or start a business. I remember many years ago, I sold half my closet on eBay and made several thousand dollars. I had no interest in starting a business on eBay, but the experience did prove to me that when there is a will, there is a way to start earning.

7. **Stop turning partners into projects.**

If you identify as the fixer or the savior in a relationship, remember that no one changes when they are forced into changing. People change when they feel motivated to change *for themselves.* So the more you try to get your partner to break a bad habit, the more they are likely to become defensive and protective about that habit. In time, you become more like their parent, and they become more like your teenage child. This dynamic destroys attraction in a relationship.

What to say to inspire change (for example, if your partner doesn't seem to be taking care of themselves the way they used to): Instead of "Why don't you ever go to the gym anymore? You need to start eating healthier." Try "I noticed you've been sleeping a lot lately. Are you feeling a bit stuck? Or sad? I'm here for you if you want to talk about it."

What to say if, no matter how hard you've tried, their intolerable habits are not changing: Instead of "If you don't stop doing _____, I can no longer be with you." Try "I really need to take care of my mental health and my well-being, and I can't do that in this relationship. So I'm moving on."

Instead of giving your partner an ultimatum, you choose yourself over fixing them.

If I'm being brutally honest, there are times when I wish I could be rescued from my problems. I think all of us, if we're really honest with ourselves, wish that it were possible for someone to come into our lives, save us from ourselves, and make us happy. For years, I actually expected that. I, just like many of you, was sold the lie that love saves the day and that with the "right" person, all my struggles would disappear. What a lie that is!

No one is coming to save us, and maybe it's time that we recognize that *this is a good thing*, not a depressing reality. When we become our own heroes (with the love and support of others), we become stronger and more resilient, and our self-esteem rises. When we learn how to access peace, purpose, and fulfillment without needing someone to give it to us, we become, slowly but surely, more whole, and we can bring that wholeness to a relationship.

___

You Must Make Peace with Your Parents

When I was twelve years old, my father insisted that I see a therapist to get to the bottom of why I was so resistant to him. He believed that "fixing" me would fix our relationship. The therapist was a serious, somewhat disheveled older man. I didn't like him at all. When he probed me to uncover my feelings about my father, I said, "It's like I'm allergic to him."

I am allergic to my father. This became my belief, my story, and part of my identity.

The story of my life, like any other, has been filled with various narratives, themes, characters, and chapters. But anyone who's had a troubled relationship with a parent knows that this troubled relationship can become the central theme of your life.

If we don't address our relationship with our parents, our romantic relationships will.

The truth was that I wasn't actually allergic to my father. I was a highly sensitive child who felt his darkness so intensely it disturbed me. Throughout my childhood, my father suffered from undiagnosed bipolar disorder. His moods were highly unpredictable, and every evening when he arrived home from work, I'd be ridden with anxiety. He was narcissistic, passive-aggressive, and abusive toward my mother. He also had a drinking and prescription drug problem. My father lived in his head—a very violent battlefield. He was rarely present; he always seemed to be far away, thinking and ruminating.

To grow up in a household with a severely emotionally dysregulated parent is traumatic for everyone in the house.

When I was alone in the apartment with my mom and sisters, I felt safe. When my father came home from work around 7 p.m., I felt unsafe. To say we walked on eggshells is an understatement. It felt more like walking on broken glass. Dad acted like a corrupt king who used his power to subordinate everyone around him. When he walked in, dinner had to be on the table, and we all had to ask him questions about his day. If we didn't focus on him, he would become irritable, hard to please, and emotionally unpredictable.

My father's whole identity was defined by being a psychiatrist. It was the only way he knew how to connect to others. He treated his family like his patients; if any of us attempted to share something that happened in our day, he'd ask, "How did that make you feel?" To this day, my body still remembers how that question made me feel. *How does it feel? It feels like I want to crawl under a rock and never have to tell you anything ever again.*

Unsurprisingly, he and my mother had a terrible marriage. They argued frequently, and I can remember a few times hearing my father, late at night from their bedroom, telling her how much she disappointed him, while I heard my mom try to defend herself and then eventually fall silent while he vented about his hurt feelings. My mother was miserable; she felt trapped and hopeless. She was a housewife without an income of her own, as well as an immigrant learning the ropes of being an American. My father was the breadwinner and had all the power.

When I was eleven years old, my parents sat me down to tell me they were divorcing and that he was moving out. I was relieved. Finally, the future seemed a little brighter for all of us.

When he was writing *The Difficult Child*, I was excited by the idea that a book was being written about me. It made me feel important and special. *A book about ME*, I remember thinking. Little did I know at the time what a huge impact it would have on my life—that being named "the difficult child" would motivate me to tirelessly prove to the world that I wasn't and that it would become the main source of my shame.

For most of my life, my troubled relationship with my father has been what a bloodstain is to a shirt: no matter how many times you try to wash it out, it remains.

One day when I was twenty-one years old, I decided to stop returning his calls. Over the next thirteen years, my father made a few attempts to reconnect, but I ignored all of them. The mere thought of a conversation with him sent waves of dread and tension throughout my entire body.

During my estrangement from my father, there were weeks, months, and even years of my life when I never consciously thought of him. It was as if he didn't exist, and so I naturally concluded that our relationship—or lack thereof—was a nonissue. But a nonissue it could never be, for the real battles we face in life are the ones we wage with ourselves, and many of the ones I confronted—particularly with my self-worth—I could always trace back to him.

It is not an accident that three significant romances in my life were with moody, passive-aggressive men with a history of drug and alcohol abuse. And one of these men, as I wrote in Truth 4, was also directly aggressive and abusive.

For years, I denied the impact that my harrowing relationship with my father had on my romantic relationships. By pretending he didn't exist, I convinced myself that all the problems I had with him would just disappear. It wasn't until my thirties that I had the self-awareness to admit to myself that living in denial of his existence wasn't helping me. I finally recognized that it took more energy to block him than to allow him back into my life some way. I decided to reestablish minimal contact with him and was able to maintain some boundaries. I reminded myself often that I was no longer a child and that if we were to have any sort of relationship, it would be on my terms. If he got snarky in some way—which he did, particularly when he didn't like something I said or if I didn't respond to his email quickly enough—my ego would take over and I'd get very defensive. If he wanted to be in my life, he would have to see that I was no longer afraid little Jillian. I was now angry, *you can't fuck with me* Jillian. If he wanted to know me, he would have to get through my stubborn ego first.

But I still felt allergic to him. My body filled with dread and rage every time I thought of him, emailed him, or saw him. I was stuck in time. Even though I was thirty-five years old, I was still seven when it came to him. It wasn't until after everything fell apart in my life that I was finally able to heal that wound.

This chapter will show you how to begin healing yours.

What happened in 2014—a miscarriage, being abandoned by my husband, followed by a divorce and the death of my mother—changed me. Becoming a relationship coach to thousands of singles and couples changed me, too. And when we change, how we see people changes, too.

I was still very aware of my father's darkness. But instead of being disturbed by it, I understood that his demons were *his* to fight, not mine. As I've become more aware of my own suffering—my internal conflicts, the shadows I run from, and my own personal demons—I can empathize with his suffering, instead of judging it or running from it. I'm an adult. He doesn't have power over me. He was older and had softened. Years ago, he acknowledged his failure as a father and was remorseful. But even if he hadn't, it would be okay. Our memories have undeniable power, and I could easily fixate on a memory from childhood that would bring my level of consciousness right back to little Jillian and hate him all over again. But I don't have to do that anymore. I don't have to protect myself anymore. I am not teenager Jillian anymore. I am no longer the twenty-one-year-old girl who decided not to return his calls for thirteen years. I choose to remain firmly in the present, in the truth of who I am, *now*. This understanding has been revelatory for my love life, and it will be for yours, too.

Your relationship with your parent doesn't have to be a troubled one for it to have had an impact on your romantic relationships. You could be very close with the person or people who raised you and still need to heal wounds that are interfering with your love life. This truth is not about how you must "choose love over fear," nor is it a happily-ever-after tale about my reconnecting with my father. It's about growing up. Our adult romantic relationships will play out the drama of our childhoods until we heal our relationship with one or both of our parents. This truth does *not* mean you reconnect with a parent who severely abused you. It does not mean you won't need boundaries with certain family members. It means that instead of viewing your parents through the eyes of your past self, you learn to see them through the eyes of your older, wiser adult self. And in doing so, you will see them differently.

How Our Caregivers Influence Our Romantic Blueprint

Sometimes we model the type of relationship(s) our parents had. Sometimes, we do the exact opposite. Sometimes, if their relationship was toxic, we say to ourselves, *That will never be me*—and we become vigilantly committed to healthy partnership.

Our caregivers influence our romantic blueprint, but it's not always a negative influence. Sometimes we will date someone who is in many ways like our mom or dad, but this isn't necessarily a bad thing. And sometimes, we will do the exact opposite. Context matters, and factors such as our social environment, work life, and physical health can all play a role. My relationship of five and a half years in my twenties had no dysfunction in it. Plus, the two relationships I had in college—although fairly short-lived—were pretty drama-free. How does this happen? It's hard to say exactly, but I do know that it's common for people to have had at least one healthy relationship even if their other relationships were not healthy. The reason in large part has to do with other stressors present in a person's life at the time the unhealthy relationship began. Why does one child, who grew up in a broken home, grow up to marry the right person and create a satisfying, lasting relationship with them, whereas another child, who comes from a stable home, can't seem to commit to anyone? As much as experts will theorize on why these things do or don't happen, we also have to acknowledge that life is often a mystery.

Most of the time, we gravitate toward what is familiar. Our subconscious chooses our partners and will often choose the ones that allow us to re-create familiar yet often dysfunctional dynamics from childhood. This doesn't mean we're all doomed. I promise that all is not lost if poor relational skills were modeled for us. Once we become aware of our patterns and address some of the issues we have because of our childhoods, we can change our relationship destiny. We can choose better, communicate better, and love better.

We are profoundly vulnerable in our romantic relationships, and as you already learned in Truth 1, our core fear of not being loved is easily triggered in them. Plus, our first teachers of love, communication, and conflict were our parents or primary caregivers. This is the reason most of us struggle in love—because our parents or caregivers likely did, too.

If you had an emotionally absent parent, as I did, when you experience a lover pulling away from you, your subconscious will likely be reminded of that scarcity, and your deepest wound of being unloved and abandoned will be triggered.

If your parents had a lot of walls and didn't freely express a lot of emotion, you might struggle to express yourself emotionally, be vulnerable, and create close romantic relationships.

If you witnessed more animosity than love between your parents, there's a chance that you either associate partnership with pain or fight a lot in your relationships, too. Or perhaps you avoid confrontation altogether and shut down instead of communicating.

If you had an emotionally immature or narcissistic parent, chances are you've dated one or more emotionally immature or even narcissistic people.

If you grew up in an alcoholic home, chances are you've fallen in love with one or more addicts.

If you were daddy's little girl, chances are no one ever lives up to daddy, or you might only date "bad boys" because you don't want to replace daddy.

If your actions rarely had consequences as a child and you could do no wrong in the eyes of mom or dad, it is possible that you have expected unconditional love from your partners, regardless of your behavior.

If you viewed your father as harsh, angry, or generally emotionally unregulated, you may have decided to become a "nice guy" so you would never be like him. This decision may have made you into a pleaser, never speaking up for what you need in a relationship.

If you were taught that the only person you can rely on is yourself, you likely have struggled to trust others, and perhaps it has been hard for you to let the love of another enter your heart.

This was Gabriela.

Girls Don't Cry

Gabriela was a very organized, responsible, hard-working, goal-oriented, achievement-focused thirty-three-year-old woman who worked in finance. She was raised in the Midwest by her strong, independent, Colombian single mom, who worked hard to provide a stellar education for her daughter. Her mother had taught Gabriela to be strong, diligent, and responsible. These are undeniably good attributes to have and were definitely great lessons for Gabriela in her professional life, but they didn't exactly help her love life.

Gabriela found me several months after she lost her mother to cancer. Her mother had always wanted her to be married, but now her mother was gone. Gabriela wanted a family of her own, but she didn't know where to go from here. The most serious relationship she'd been in had lasted only six months.

At our first meeting, Gabriela said, "My mom once told me, 'Girls don't cry,' so I try not to let myself feel too much . . . or get out of control."

I was shocked by what she said. I had heard the (ridiculous) phrase "boys don't cry," but I'd never heard of a girl being told that *girls don't cry*.

Vulnerability is, in many ways, a superpower, and yet instead of encouraging children to connect to their emotional selves, society tells them that vulnerability is weakness. Women have a natural inclination toward connecting to our more intuitive, emotional selves, but Gabriela was completely divorced from this part of herself, and it was impacting her ability to have a loving romantic relationship. She believed that in order to be strong, responsible, and resilient, she had to reject all the vulnerabilities—such as softness, openness, and the willingness to lean on others for support—that are necessary to build intimacy with another person. Boundaries are one thing, but Gabriela had surrounded herself with iron walls. Walls imprison us.

When I observed Gabriela, I could see she felt emotional but was fighting every urge she had to cry. I could see her grief in her eyes and in the way her shoulders rounded forward and down. I could see the tension around the corners of her mouth—a pattern I saw frequently in people who clenched their jaws. Gabriela was very controlled, stoic, and tense. Controlling her feelings so she could appear invulnerable was a learned behavior that I knew was significantly detrimental to her well-being.

"That must be very challenging for you in your relationships with men—not being able to express how you feel," I said.

"With my ex-boyfriend, we didn't really go that deep with each other. I mean, it's not that I didn't want to. I always felt like something was missing, but I couldn't put my finger on it."

I told her I wasn't surprised to hear that. Then I said, "I believe your mom told you that girls don't cry because her intention was to protect you from a world she believed would take advantage of you if you weren't strong and successful."

"Yes, I believe that."

"Good," I said. "So now that you have proven that you *are* responsible and have achieved a lot of career success, perhaps now we should focus on helping you find balance so you can feel joy, love, and freedom, too."

She smiled sheepishly. "That sounds nice. But how?"

"If your mom knew how guarded you were in your relationships, do you think she'd be happy?"

"No. In fact, she always wanted me to get married and have a family. She never understood why my last two relationships ended after a few months. I guess we both figured I didn't meet the right person yet."

I go deep quickly with clients. During our two-hour session, I wanted to go deeper with Gabriela. But before I did, I had to ask her an important question. I never want to project my spiritual beliefs onto a client. I first want to know what their spiritual or religious beliefs are, if any, and then I coach them based on their beliefs—if applicable.

"I'm curious, Gabriela, do you believe your mom can still see and observe you? In other words, do you believe her energy is still present around you?"

"Yes," she answered very definitively.

"What do you think her message would be to you?"

"Well, I know she wants me to meet a really great guy, get married, and start a family—which is what I really want, too," she said, as if to reassure me that her dreams were aligned with her mother's.

"What do you think she would tell you that you need to do to make that happen for yourself?" I asked, gently looking into Gabriela's eyes.

She looked up, searching her brain for an answer. "I think she would tell me to stop being so uptight." She chuckled a little. "And to stop worrying so much about my to-do lists and my job performance—I mean, I think she would want me to still focus on work but to be easier on myself."

This was a critical moment in my conversation with Gabriela. For most of her life, she believed that in order to be enough for her mother, she had to be the girl who doesn't cry—who is invulnerable to the unfairness and harshness of the world. Her mother, based on her own experiences in the world as a single mom and also an immigrant, innocently conditioned Gabriela to overdevelop qualities such as independence and ambition and to underdevelop qualities such as ease and sensitivity. To acknowledge that her mother would want Gabriela to "stop being so uptight" and to "stop worrying" was significant. It meant that Gabriela could begin to let go of having to be so rigid and controlled.

Since my own mother died, I've had many moments when I've thought, *Mom would be so disappointed with me* if I did this or didn't do that. I realized that I was still making many of my decisions based on what *she* would have wanted, and when I didn't do what I thought she would have wanted me to do, I'd feel enormous shame. Even after her passing, I was still searching for her approval.

In many ways, though, I feel closer to my mom now that she is gone than when she was here. This was a very unexpected discovery for me. We were always close; she was the safe harbor in the storm with my father. But we still had typical mother-daughter arguments, and there were still aspects of my mother that I would sometimes find annoying or even hurtful. But with her passing, there are no more opportunities to get annoyed at her or to have typical mother-daughter fights. All that's left is love.

After the death of a parent, your rebellious self might think, *Oh, Mom is no longer here. I am fully autonomous. I can do whatever I want! I don't have to hear unsolicited advice from the peanut gallery!* On the other hand, you still feel tethered to your parent and want to please them.

But so many of us forget that our parents (with rare exception) just want us to be safe and happy. Their desires for us are not about being perfect, creating the perfect family, or making a million dollars. Are you on a path that's authentic and fulfilling to you? Because that's ultimately what parents want: for their children's core needs to be fulfilled, for them to have a strong moral compass, and for them to become respectable members of society.

I needed to help Gabriela develop a wiser perspective on her mother. "Why do you think your mom said, 'Girls don't cry'?" I asked. "Had she known that saying that to you would create so many walls around you, do you think she still would have said that?"

"No," Gabriela quickly replied.

"So why do you think she said that?"

"Because she wanted to make sure I survived?"

Ding, ding, ding! Bingo. Gabriela was on the precipice of a breakthrough, and I couldn't have been more excited about it.

Gabriela's mom was an impressive prototype of the American dream. She came to the United States alone at twenty years old and immediately started cleaning people's homes in order to live in her tiny cubicle of an apartment in Florida. Within seven years, she had started her own housekeeping company, which then became one of the top housekeeping companies in Florida, with five offices. Telling Gabriela that "girls don't cry" was her mother's attempt to help Gabriela be the strongest, most capable person she could be. Her mother was trying to help Gabriela keep the world from swallowing her.

"That's right," I told Gabriela. "Those words your mother said to you had so much impact, they practically shaped who you are, Gabriela. But our job as adults is to investigate the meaning behind the words that impact us so that maybe we can stop taking them so literally. We have to understand the context that surrounds them. Does this make sense?"

"Yes, it does. Wow. It's crazy how much that affected me. I didn't really remember it until we started speaking."

Gabriela shared with me that three different men had given her similar feedback. They each told her that it felt really hard to read her and that they felt they were being kept at arm's length. They could never really tell how she felt about them, and it was hard to get close to her.

I couldn't help but think to myself that Gabriela was the emotionally unavailable guy so many of my clients and social media followers complain about. She was like a stoic man on the outside, but what I was able to see inside her was an incredibly vulnerable woman who longed for love and a family of her own. That was her main internal conflict, and her mom's passing was an opportunity for Gabriela to find her autonomy while building a relationship with her mom's spirit, who really just wanted the best for her.

I took the risk of injecting a little humor into our conversation when I said, "It's almost as if you're the emotionally unavailable guy!"

It landed well, thankfully.

"OMG. You're so right. Ha! Here I thought *they* were emotionally unavailable!" she said excitedly.

"Gabriela, you can take the best parts of your mom, but you don't have to be your mom. Your circumstances are very different from hers. You don't *have* to be so tough on yourself to survive. You can be very ambitious and also be vulnerable and let yourself cry."

Many times throughout our sessions together, I would watch Gabriela fight hard to hold back her tears, particularly when she was talking about her mother. This session was no different. The moment I told her that she didn't have to be her mother—that she didn't have to choose between being ambitious and being vulnerable—I could see her body start to let go of the years of tension it had been holding on to. Her shoulders relaxed, and I could see her jaw loosen. The tears started to well up in her eyes.

"You can let go, Gabriela. You can cry, and when you do, you're going to feel so much better. You're going to feel so relaxed afterward. All that tension in your neck and your shoulders is going to melt away. Crying is just letting go of that stuck energy that desperately wants to be free," I said, compassionately.

And so she cried.

Gabriela and I worked together for about five months. I remember in between sessions she would write me and say, "I had a really good cry today ☺."

And I would respond: "That's great! What do you think your mom would think about that?"

"I think she would feel happy that I feel happy doing it."

Changing the Story

We need to break up with our parents as the leaders of our belief systems in order to save or even improve our relationship with them. Most of us are moving through life like the walking wounded, unconsciously controlled by the need to seek our parents' approval. This isn't about blaming our parents. This is about the child who lives within all of us, who is still, in adulthood, living life unconsciously under the influence of their parental conditioning. Some of that conditioning is positive, such as learning to be polite to strangers. Maybe your parents conditioned you to have a great work ethic. Maybe you saw your parents put family first, and that's really important to you, to see the world through the lens of family.

Not all conditioning is "bad." The aim is to be aware of what you want to keep versus what has been sabotaging your chances at feeling more whole. When we break up with our parents as the sovereigns of our beliefs, we get back together with the parts of ourselves we never thought we "should" be. We give ourselves permission to be whole—to be authentic. From a place of authenticity, we can love our parents as adults, not as children in need. We can respect our parents without needing to please them. If needed, we set boundaries.

When we do this, we grow up, and our relationships grow up, too.

For Gabriela to feel more whole and true to who she was, she needed to break up with her story about who she thought she had to be. As long as Gabriela divorced herself from her vulnerability, she would continue to silently suffer, wondering why she couldn't have what she so deeply desired: partnership and a family of her own. It's not that she was wrong for believing what she believed. Her mother was Gabriela's hero. They were incredibly close. If her mom told her that girls don't cry because they had to be strong, courageous, and independent, that is what Gabriela would become. But the story had to be investigated with a different lens. Gabriela had to put herself in her mother's shoes and understand *why* her mother said that, to understand the bigger picture. To reclaim the lost parts of herself, Gabriela had to give the story a different meaning and to recognize what her mother would say differently today. Gabriela had to individuate herself from her beloved mother and reconnect with her own authentic self.

As adults, it begins with us. If we want to heal—particularly our romantic relationships—we have a responsibility to look at our pasts through the eyes of our wiser, mature selves. We have to become curious and investigate. Most of the time, our parents are like strangers to us. Even if we were close to them, rarely do we as their child ask our parents about their dreams, deepest longings, and regrets—or even about the time they first fell in love or got into trouble. Instead, we see our parents through the filter of our much younger selves.

Weeks before writing this chapter, I lost my father.

Before he died, I'd reached a significant place in my healing with him, but when he died, I was ashamed that I hadn't been able to transcend my ego and fear even more, and build an even stronger relationship with him. Thankfully though, I've been able to give myself grace. I did the best that I could. There is also a part of me that feels a little bit relieved that I don't have to remember to *call Dad today.* The trajectory of healing and letting go is a process, and I'm still going through it with my father.

I'm so incredibly different from my father. I don't battle mental illness. I may have selfish tendencies, as we all do, but I'm not a narcissist. I'm also not an immigrant from Poland who narrowly escaped Nazi control as an infant. Nonetheless, it is not lost on me that my path parallels his in some way. Although I am not a psychiatrist, I am a coach with extensive training in psychology who helps people heal. My father wrote books about his field, as I am now doing, too. We can reject our parents as much as we want, but it won't change the fact that the apple never falls far from the tree.

Even though most people could validate me for hating my father, the greatest truth is that I would not be where I am today, writing this book and hopefully helping you, if it weren't for my past and my relationship with him. So, I can stay tethered to a story that imprisons me in my resentment, fear, and tension, or I can accept that my suffering had a deeper purpose. I can change what it all means, and by doing so, I can change the story.

A big sign of my personal growth is that I do not date men anymore who are similar to the worst parts of my father. I don't date men who represent any part of my struggle with my childhood anymore. If you shut down, if you're passive-aggressive, if you struggle with drugs or alcohol, if you can't regulate your emotions, you do not get a ticket to enter my life. That pattern is broken. And I broke it by making peace with my parents and by practicing everything in this book.

. . . .

PRACTICING THIS TRUTH

Finding Peace with Our Parents

Finding peace with a difficult parent doesn't mean that every wound is healed and now you can have a wonderful relationship. It also doesn't mean you have to love your parent(s) to find peace with who they are or are not. Even if they have passed away or you never met this parent, you can still find peace.

Step 1: Grieve the Parent You Never Had

In order to make room for a calmer, more peaceful relationship with a parent (even if you never see them), first grieve the parent you wished they had been to you. All of us, including our parents and *their* parents, deserve healthy, loving caregivers. But we don't always receive what we deserve. We have to accept the fact that we didn't have the parent(s) we deserved because they didn't either. We do so by grieving: feeling our feelings, maybe writing them all down, letting the pain come in, and then letting it go—as many times as we need to. I still have moments when I grieve the father I wished I'd had. What helps now is to remember that not having what I deserved gave me what I needed to grow. I wouldn't be here today, writing this book, if I'd had the father I always wanted.

Step 2: Be Open to Looking at Your Parent(s) Differently

Finding peace with our parents has very little to do with them and everything to do with the story of them, specifically the story of us and them. Every memory we have of them is like a scene from a movie or a page from a chapter that cannot be erased. That's because stories do not die. Our interpretations, though, can entirely change the arc of a story. Many people, including me until I started to heal, are haunted by the stories of their past, and these stories serve as powerful yet negative reference points for our lives as adults. When we recall our parents and childhoods, we are replaying the same memories we've had since we were very young. In doing so, certain thoughts are reinforced—for example, *They never change*; *They are so f*cked up*; *They f*cked me up*; *They should have known better*; *How dare they?*; *They didn't care about me*; *If they loved me they wouldn't have . . .* ; and so on. Then what we're left with is more rage, more sadness, and more hopelessness. More trauma. More repetitions of the negative cycles we re-create in our relationships.

To change the way we look at the story, we have to change the way we look at our parent(s). As children, we didn't see our parents as human; we saw them as superhuman. As we get older, instead of seeing them as fallible humans doing the best they can, we still, unconsciously, expect them to be superhuman—to be perfectly safe and selfless and to be our protectors. It's time to see our parents through the filter of our wiser adult self, and no longer from the perspective of our vulnerable and dependent child self.

Here are ten questions to ask your wiser adult self so that you can see your parents differently:

1. Do I understand why they are the way they are?

2. How would seeing them differently help my love life today?

3. What does my story about them give me? Does it validate me? Does it help me bond with other members of the family? Does it make me feel justified?

4. What part of me is just like them? How have I been rejecting, if at all, the part of me that is like them?

5. Is it possible they have no idea of the impact they have had on me and others?

6. Is my perspective of them influenced by another family member?

7. How have they suffered? What was their childhood like?

8. Am I resilient and strong because of them? Did I inherit some of their gifts?

9. What current expectations do I have for my relationship with them that I need to let go of?

10. Is it possible they have changed at all? Is it possible that what I believe about them might be misinformed or outdated?

Step 3: If Possible, Have a Conversation with Your Parent(s)

As we saw in Truth 5, most of us go through life avoiding uncomfortable conversations. It may not be possible or safe for you to have a conversation with your mother or father—in which case, you must not. But if it *is* possible and safe, I recommend that you have a conversation with one or both of them about their experiences. Can you talk with them from a place of curiosity? The point of the conversation is to understand who they are, beyond their identity as your mom or dad. You can ask them about their childhoods, their goals, their fondest memories, and maybe even their hardest memories. The following are some examples of questions to ask your parents:

1. What was your relationship like with your parents?

2. How was love expressed in the home you grew up in?

3. How were you punished?

4. What was your favorite hobby as a child?

5. What's your biggest regret?

6. Do you wish you had pursued a different career or life path?

7. When was the last time you really enjoyed yourself, and why?

8. When was the first time you fell in love? When was the first time you got your heart broken?

9. What is most important to you, and has that changed over the years?

A Note About Boundaries

The first stage of healing my relationship with my father was by having boundaries with him. I was no longer a child who didn't have a voice. If you have felt voiceless in your relationship with one or both of your parents, it is crucial that you remember you are not helpless anymore. Part of relating to your parents as adults is by being an adult yourself. You do not have to be afraid to enforce guidelines for how you want to be treated and boundaries around what you can or cannot do for them. But the final destination is a place where your ego isn't really involved anymore. You don't take things personally. It doesn't mean letting go of all boundaries, but you don't have to be so defensive.

A *note to those who suffered physical or sexual abuse from a caregiver*: You do not have to forgive your caregiver. They don't deserve your forgiveness. My hope, though, is that you start seeing *yourself* through a different lens. You are not only a survivor. You are also a hero. Anyone who has had to overcome such horrendous trauma is the most courageous person of all.

A note for those who are in a relationship: It doesn't matter what your childhood was like or how well suited you and your partner are; you will still trigger each other. Hopefully, you won't do so frequently, but it will happen. Awareness is key. You must know what trauma your partner lives with and then commit to not being a continuation of the story that has caused them pain. In other words, as conscious people in a relationship, you must aim to do your best to not retraumatize each other. For example, if their mother pulled away a lot, then you must be very conscious that you don't pull away, too. If their father was controlling, then you must do everything you can to not be controlling, too—even if that has been your pattern in former relationships.

After my father died, I found photos of him I'd never seen in my life, and there was one in particular that struck me. It was him, around my age, in pigeon pose. He had never talked to me about yoga, so I was shocked to see him doing a common yoga pose that stretches the hips. I saw how much I looked like him—how much my long limbs, which I had always thought were more like my mother's, were more like his. His pigeon pose was eerily similar to my own. It was a tender and humbling moment for me to realize that perhaps there was more to this man than just a difficult father or a bad husband. There was another human being trying to do the best he could and to hold it, and their pigeon, together. And I was more like him than I had realized.

It's Never Too Late to Choose Yourself

If you had met me in my thirties, you would never have thought I was a person with relationship issues. I had no problems marching to the beat of my own drum. I had solid friendships and drama-free relationships, including a very loving relationship in my twenties that lasted over five years.

But as you learned, I was also in an abusive relationship. I was in situationships where I chased unavailable men because I wanted so badly to be loved and partnered. I used to think that I lost my way once I got married, when in truth, I had started to lose my way before I even met my ex-husband. I felt unfulfilled. I didn't know what I wanted out of life, but I did know that I, just like all of us, wanted love. When I got married in my late thirties, I became a prisoner of my limitations. I believed that my relationship with my ex was more important than my relationship with myself and consequently betrayed myself several times to keep the peace. I didn't have the tools to communicate well when things got tough between us. I also didn't know how to ask for what I needed—because I had no idea asking for what you need was even a thing one does in a relationship! I also couldn't put my needs aside to listen to *him* when *he* was upset, because I felt like a constant victim. I didn't have the courage to leave a relationship that was clearly not working because in my view, "divorce" was a bad word. If I was divorced, I was a loser. I also couldn't leave because I felt I had nothing without him.

These were my limitations.

I made being in a relationship my full-time job; teaching yoga was something I did on the side. I lost my way, and I often felt like a little girl trapped in a woman's body. The end of my relationship plus the death of my mom forced me to grow up quickly, however; that's when I turned it all around and finally chose myself. But remember, you don't need a tragedy or a breakup to wake you up. All you need is the willingness to look within.

Some people need to make their work *less* important and focus more on loving their partner well. For me, the task was really finding my voice in the world. After my divorce, I made the decision that I wasn't going to pursue motherhood. This was a very hard decision that forced me to grieve the path that I and society had always expected I would walk. But life had different plans for me, and something inside of me knew that choosing myself meant going in a new direction.

I studied relationships because I wanted to be as prepared as I possibly could be for my next one. In the past, I'd thought that once time passed after a breakup, I'd find a partner and be happy. But even though time helps to heal pain, it doesn't break patterns. I recognized that it wasn't just about time or finding a new partner. I also had to change. I wanted to know not only how to choose a partner well but also how to create a better relationship, starting with myself.

If I had more skills, then I'd attract someone with more skills, too. Like attracts like. Water seeks its own level. We tend to gravitate toward someone with a similar level of consciousness as our own.

What I needed to do was not only to learn about my attachment style but also how to love myself—and how to love another with less ego. I had work to do, and everything I learned I taught to others, which taught me even more.

I wasn't raised to follow my dreams. I was more the kind of girl who would easily abandon her dreams and follow her boyfriend instead. For much of my life, I had been filled with a lot of fear, doubt, and uncertainty, so choosing myself meant figuring out how to cultivate safety and certainty within myself. This meant finally walking away from teaching yoga as my full-time job and starting a new career teaching people about love. It meant pouring all my focus into building my self-worth. I did this by meeting my needs. I went back to school so I could become a coach. I needed more financial independence, so I worked my ass off to become an entrepreneur, even though I had never thought that would be possible for me. I nurtured my friendships so that I could feel more love and connection in my life that was unrelated to romance. I read dozens of books and attended weeklong seminars. I wanted to write even though I had never written before, so I started a newsletter where I shared everything I knew about people, love, and relationships.

All along the way, I kept looking within with the intent to understand myself, forgive myself, and break patterns that were no longer serving me.

My heart was shattered in 2014, but I needed to make the catastrophe mean something other than that my life was over. I had to make it mean that my life was beginning.

My parents didn't model the skills for a healthy relationship. They also didn't model healthy self-esteem. So I taught myself, with the help of incredible mentors and brilliant experts whose teachings I devoured. My students and clients also became my teachers. By integrating the nine truths into my life, I made myself more whole.

Today, I am far from perfect, but I choose myself, and I know that I am worth it. I know what healthy love is, and I know what self-love is, even though I can still sometimes be hard on myself. I know what demons I face, but I am not so naive as to believe that I am the only one who *has* demons to face.

Lots of people grow old, but not all of them grow wise.

I don't see my mistakes as failures, I see them as wisdom. If you run away from your mistakes, you'll always be miserably repeating the same patterns. But if you're willing to pay attention to what your mistakes were trying to teach you, you get to wear them as badges of honor, because they're the lessons that forced you to evolve into a better person. Learn the lessons, as I did. You don't have to be afraid of your mom or dad. You don't have to please your way to love. You don't have to play that game you've been playing anymore. You can choose a better way. Just by reading this book, you've changed. You've developed a deeper awareness and a stronger character.

Choosing Yourself

You do not have to be completely healed to have a happy, secure relationship. Each one of us is a work in progress. But you do have to finally choose yourself—and this applies to everyone, whether you're single, dating, or in a partnership.

Choosing yourself is not necessarily about choosing to be single—although it can be. For example, a lot of people choose to be single for a period of time because they've been in unhealthy relationships and they want to work on themselves and break patterns.

But choosing yourself is not about reacting to someone who's wronged you and making them the villain. Choosing yourself is the decision to live your life with as much authenticity and integrity as possible. Ultimately, choosing yourself is about becoming the hero of your story.

Choosing yourself is committing yourself to the life you know you must lead, even if it's not what your parents wanted or what society has told you to do.

Choosing yourself means deciding to learn new skills so that you can cocreate the relationship you want and deserve.

Choosing yourself is making a conscious effort to behave as your higher self in your relationships as much as possible.

Choosing yourself means walking away from unhealthy people and relationships and demanding more for your life.

Choosing yourself means sitting with your discomfort when you would rather run away, avoid, or control.

Choosing yourself is when you pause instead of reacting.

Choosing yourself is not letting what society has told you about age stop you from truly living. It's getting divorced at forty, married at fifty, and pursuing your dreams at sixty.

Choosing yourself is learning how to take care of yourself emotionally and financially when you never thought that you could or were never taught how.

Choosing yourself is giving yourself permission to move on after heartbreak.

Choosing yourself is having the hard conversations when all you've ever known is keeping the peace.

Choosing yourself is refusing to jump through hoops trying to prove your value to someone.

Choosing yourself is asserting yourself with firmness, not harshness.

Choosing yourself is climbing the mountain.

Choosing yourself is being yourself, not who you think your partner or date wants you to be.

Choosing yourself is loving someone when you want to punish them.

Choosing yourself means being compassionate toward yourself.

Choosing yourself is taking the risk to be vulnerable.

Choosing yourself is no longer chasing unavailable people and instead chasing your dreams.

By reading this book, you chose yourself.

Regardless of your trauma, your relationship history, whether you're in a relationship right now or not, you can turn it all around. It really does begin with you. You can do it. You can't believe those thoughts that tell you that it's too late for you or that you're not good enough.

When you reflect on your love life and all your past relationships, what is the story you tell yourself? Is your story filled with anguish, or does it have any hope? How many villains are there in your story? How many victims? Which one are you?

Most people, when they come to me, don't feel empowered in their love lives. Instead, they feel stuck, frustrated, and fearful. Just like me years ago, they don't understand why the same issues keep resurfacing that prevent them from having the relationship they want. Unfortunately, many arrive at the conclusion that they're just not good at love or they're simply unlovable.

Truth is, many of us struggle in our love lives, but anyone who is willing can learn how to thrive. Painful relationships, dates that never form into real relationships, or just unfulfilling love do *not* have to be a part of one's destiny. You're so much more powerful than you realize. Truly what's standing in the way is you. You don't have to be perfect. You're still going to mess up. This is about progress, about being totally honest with yourself, about being honest with others, and about being accountable.

In order to rewrite the story of your love life, you must first be willing to look within. There's no force out there that wants to deny you love. You're not paying off karmic debt, and you're not being punished by the universe. You just have to be willing to make some changes to the way you've been approaching romantic relationships. These changes begin with your understanding and integration of the nine truths:

1. It begins with you. "They" do not have the power. We do.
   All the disappointment, confusion, and drama of your former relationships can be traced to the universal fear that you're not enough.

2. Our minds are always creating stories, and if we don't question our thoughts and beliefs, our heads can quickly become battlefields.

3. Lust is not love, and knowing the difference is essential for building long-lasting love.

4. Self-love *is* actually all that it's cracked up to be. We need it to thrive in a relationship.

5. We have to speak up and tell the truth. If we hide what we see, feel, or need, a relationship will deteriorate quickly.

6. Stress and fear can turn a secure relationship into a dysfunctional

one. We need to make it a priority to show up as our higher selves as much as possible.

7. As much as we may try, we cannot convince anyone to love us.

8. Happiness is an inside job, and there's no perfect person out there who is going to rescue us from ourselves.

9. And finally, if we don't address our childhoods, our romantic relationships will. We have to learn how to relate to our parents from the perspective of wise adults, not wounded children.

None of us was given a handbook for living. All of us are doing the best that we can to be enough and to be happy. It takes a lot of courage to look within, and the moment you do is the moment you take the first step as the hero of your own story. It begins with you.

Acknowledgments

Life, along with all the relationships we will have in it, is a classroom, and we are all students and teachers. I've been lucky in my own life to have incredible teachers, and it is my privilege to pass on the knowledge I've learned throughout the years. My greatest teachers have been my students and clients over the past twenty-one years; I will be forever grateful to them for showing me how to become a better teacher. I promise each and every one of you to continue to voraciously study so that I keep growing and evolving into a better teacher for all of you.

To my global community, the Conscious Woman: Thank you all for working so hard to love yourselves and for humbly looking in the mirror and growing. Thank you for putting your trust in me and being a light and support for everyone in the community.

To my family: Thank you to my sisters, Janice and Debra, for being the best big sisters anyone could ask for, even when I wasn't the best little sister. Life has always felt less lonely knowing I had you both in my corner.

To my beloved stepfather: Thank you for showing us safety. To my father: I hope you are finally at peace.

Mom, you are always with me.

Thank you to my coach, Delaine, who has been by my side since the beginning. I am forever grateful to you for believing in me when I wanted to give up—which was often—and for providing me with invaluable advice, resources, and the clear direction I needed to be able to do what I do today.

To my mentors Tony Robbins and Cloé Madanes: Thank you, Tony, for being a shining light in my darkest moments and for inspiring me to help people in ways I never thought possible. My whole life changed when I went to your live events, Unleash the Power Within and Date with Destiny, and I will forever be your student. And thank you, Cloé: your brilliance has taught me how to truly understand people and, thus, help them change.

Thank you to my book coach, Leigh Stein. Without you, Leigh, I would have given up on this book a long time ago. Thank you for being my biggest support in writing *It Begins with You* and for helping me get twenty years of information in my brain down onto the page. I am so lucky to have you. Thank you, also, Emily Stone, for encouraging me to write this book and for all your sound advice.

Thank you to my first book coach, Joelle Hann. Not only did you teach me how to write a proposal, but you planted the seed years ago that I should write a book. Your influence will never be forgotten.

Thank you to my team at HarperOne, especially Anna Paustenbach, Chantal Tom, and Gabriella Page-Fort, and to my fantastic agents, Sarah Passick and Mia Vitale. I'm so grateful to you all for believing in this book and my vision, and for lifting me up in times of doubt.

Thank you to my publicist, Nicole Perez Krueger, and the whole wonderful team at Align PR for supporting me and my growth.

Thank you to Steve Wilson, David Henning, Rob Herting, Will Tendy, Shin Yin Hiyu, Lily McIntyre, and Rian Kountzhouse of QCODE, for making my podcast, *Jillian on Love*, a reality, and for giving me a platform to teach and help people.

In many ways it all began with Kula Yoga Project in New York City, where I first became a yoga teacher. Kula is forever in my heart, my home away from home, and my memories there are some of the best memories of my life. To Schuyler Grant, Nikki Vilella, and Nikki Costello: thank you for making me sweat, for helping me feel at home in my body, and for giving me the gift of teaching.

Thank you to all my closest girlfriends (you know who you are) for supporting me over the years and always being there for me.

To my ex-husband: Our relationship was at times the best I had ever had—and the worst. Our relationship woke me up, and it led me here. You said we were on different paths, and even though I didn't know what the hell you meant back then, you could not have been more right.